CRASH COURSE
FOR THE GMAT

THE PRINCETON REVIEW

CRASH COURSE FOR THE GMAT

The Last-Minute Guide to Scoring High

by Cathryn Still

Random House
New York

Princeton Review Publishing, L.L.C.
2315 Broadway
New York, NY 10024
E-mail: comments@review.com

Published in the United States by Random House, Inc., New York, and
simultaneously in Canada by Random House of Canada Limited, Toronto.

ISBN 0-375-75618-3

Editor: Rachel Warren
Designer: Stephanie Martin
Production Editor: Maria Dente
Production Coordinator: Stephanie Martin

Manufactured in the United States of America.

9   8   7   6   5   4   3   2   1

ACKNOWLEDGMENTS

The Princeton Review's GMAT course, a primary source for this book, would not be the powerhouse it is without the help and guidance of these smart, committed people: Tim Wheeler, Dan Edmonds, Susan Baer, Jack Schieffer, and Magda Pecsenye. We would like to acknowledge the original team of teachers and developers who conceived and brought our first GMAT course to life: Alicia Ernst, Tom Meltzer, Paul Foglino, John Sheehan, Mark Sawula, Nell Goddin, Teresa Connelly, and Philip Yee. We also thank all the people involved in the production of this book: Rachel Warren for her editing expertise, Stephanie Martin for her production talents, and Maria Dente for handling the details.

A big round of applause goes out to our students: Your hard work and tough questions are the reasons we love what we do. Finally, the author would like to personally thank her family and her sweetheart, David, for their love and support.

CONTENTS

PART I

INTRODUCTION

ORIENTATION

WHAT IS A CRASH COURSE?

So the GMAT is coming up fast, and all your best intentions of studying an hour a day for the past three months have gone out the window. Not to worry—there's still hope. *Crash Course for the GMAT* will give you an effective strategy for tackling the GMAT, even though you're down to the wire. After a brief overview of the format of the entire GMAT, we'll dive right into a 10-step study plan designed to give you the highest possible rate of return. We've broken down each section by question type, and identified the best strategy for each type of question you'll see on the exam. But *Crash Course for the GMAT* is not a comprehensive study guide for the GMAT—if you have more time and that's what you're looking for, try The Princeton Review's *Cracking the GMAT*, by Geoff Martz.

WHAT IS THE GMAT?

The Graduate Management Admissions Test (GMAT) is primarily intended to measure the aptitude of applicants to Masters of Business Administration programs. This multiple-choice ordeal is not an indicator of intelligence, nor will it in any way predict your grades in business school or the likelihood that you'll sell your start-up for $50 million three years out. It's just a measure of how well you perform on standardized tests.

The GMAT is made up of two parts: an Analytical Writing Assessment (AWA) and a multiple-choice portion with two sections, Verbal and Quantitative. The Analytical Writing Assessment consists of two, type-written, 30-minute essays. The first essay, called Analysis of an Issue, asks you to choose and defend one side of a dilemma, while the second essay, Analysis of an Argument, requires you to critique the author's position on a particular dilemma or argument.

The 75-minute Verbal section of the GMAT consists of 41 multiple-choice questions, 11 of which are experimental (not scored). We'll tell you more about the experimental questions later. In this section, you'll see three types of questions (in no particular order):

- Reading comprehension (approximately 14 questions and 4 passages)
- Sentence correction (approximately 14 questions)
- Logical reasoning (approximately 14 questions)

The 75-minute Quantitative (math) section of the GMAT contains 37 questions of two types (again, in no particular order):

- Problem solving (18-22 questions)
- Data sufficiency (15-19 questions)

WHO WRITES THE GMAT?

The GMAT is the brainchild of Education Testing Services (ETS), the folks who brought you the SAT in high school, and who write a smorgasbord of other standardized tests, ranging from tests for pro golfers to the Series 7. This enormous, near-monopolistic, tax-exempt private corporation is based in New Jersey. It produces the GMAT under the sponsorship of the Graduate Management Admission Council (GMAC), a board composed of top b-school admissions officers and deans who set standards for admissions to accredited business schools in the United States.

HOW'S IT SCORED?

Your GMAT scores will be broken down into two separate scores, one for the AWA and another for the multiple-choice portion of the test. The AWA essays are each graded holistically on a scale of 0 (unintelligible) to 6 (well done), and then the two essays' scores are averaged to generate your overall AWA score, on the same scale.

Your performance on each multiple-choice section of the test will generate a two-digit number, called the sectional subscore, ranging from 0–60. These two subscores are combined into a three-digit number, called your composite, or overall, score. Overall scores range from 200–800. A score of 500 is considered average (50th percentile), while a score of 650 would put you in the 90th percentile.

Scores on the AWA and the multiple-choice portion of the tests are separate—they do not affect each other in any way.

EXPERIMENTAL QUESTIONS

Scattered throughout the Verbal and Quantitative sections of the test are approximately 18 questions that do not count toward your score.

These are experimental, or research questions, and their sole purpose is to generate data for ETS. You will not recognize the experimental questions; they look and feel just like the real thing. ETS uses your performance on these questions to determine their viability and to generate scoring statistics on them. In essence, ETS is using you as a lab rat on a test you're paying them a lot of money to take!

WHAT DO YOU GUYS KNOW, ANYWAY?

The Princeton Review has been monitoring the GMAT for years. Our teaching methods were developed and are continually honed through regular, detailed analyses of the topics tested on the GMAT, and *how* these topics are tested. We teach strategies that allow you to quickly discern the most efficient and safest path to take in answering questions, and techniques that help you take control of the testing structure and environment, and even use them to your advantage.

HOW TO REGISTER

The GMAT is given, by appointment only, in computer testing centers. While theoretically you could call at any time and arrange to take the test the next day (the GMAT is administered nearly every day of the month), it's best to call well ahead of when you wish to sit for the test. During peak times (October through March), testing appointments may fill several weeks in advance.

To schedule your GMAT testing session, call 800-GMAT-NOW. The test costs $125, and to complete your registration by telephone, you'll have to pay by credit card. You can also find out more about the test at www.gmat.org, or by calling 609-771-7330.

While your score for the multiple-choice section is available almost immediately after taking the test, b-schools require you to file an official score report, which is typically released by ETS two to four weeks later. Make sure you are scheduling your GMAT test far enough ahead of your application deadlines for your schools to receive your official scores.

COMPUTER ADAPTIVE? WHAT ON EARTH DOES THAT MEAN?

The GMAT is what's known as a Computer Adaptive Test, or CAT. What this means, in part, is that the order of the questions in the multiple-choice portions of the test are not determined in advance; rather, each new question you see is determined by your performance on the question that preceded it.

WHAT WILL THE TEST LOOK LIKE?

Your GMAT will start out with an untimed tutorial in which you'll learn how to use a mouse, how to scroll, how to type your AWA, and what the various icons that appear throughout the test mean. Once you have completed the tutorial, you'll take your AWA. Then, after a short break, your multiple-choice test begins.

Each section will begin with an instruction screen for the type of question you are about to see. These instruction screens are timed, so don't spend any time reading them—you'll know all you need to know about them by the time you finish this book. Here's what a sample question looks like on screen:

Section 1	35:00	Question 2 of 25

Art teacher: Art students are less talented and show less creativity today than they used to. The work my students have done this semester shows a lack of both creativity and skill.

Which one of the following is the most serious weakness in the argument made by the teacher?

○ It does not show that the decline in talent among the teacher's students is representative of a decline in talent among art students in general.

○ It does not prove that the teacher is a good judge of artistic talent as displayed by students.

○ It fails to consider the possibility that the art teacher is not a good instructor.

○ It fails to present evidence which may contradict its conclusion.

○ The terms used in the teacher's argument are not sufficiently defined.

During the test, the following icons will appear:

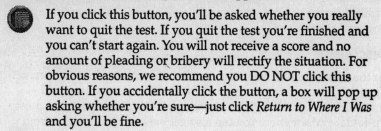

If you click this button, you'll be asked whether you really want to quit the test. If you quit the test you're finished and you can't start again. You will not receive a score and no amount of pleading or bribery will rectify the situation. For obvious reasons, we recommend you DO NOT click this button. If you accidentally click the button, a box will pop up asking whether you're sure—just click *Return to Where I Was* and you'll be fine.

If you click this button you will exit the section you're currently working on, and you won't get a score on it. If you finish a section before time runs out, just sit there and wait. You can't end early by clicking this button.

Finally, a button you can use. By clicking the clock icon, you can make the digital timer appear (if it's hidden) or go away (if it's visible). It's up to you. Either way, in the last five minutes of the test, the timer will appear on your screen and start flashing.

All this button does is remind you of the instructions for the question type you're working on. Pretty useless.

When you've selected an answer for the question you're working on, click *Next*. This will take you to the *Answer Confirm* screen.

ETS wants you to be absolutely sure of each answer you've chosen, so each time you answer a question and click *Next Question*, you'll see an *Answer Confirm* screen. It looks just like the screen before it, except that the *Answer Confirm* button is highlighted, and the *Next* button is grayed out. If you're sure the answer choice you've selected is the one you want, click *Answer Confirm* and you'll proceed to the next question.

REAL TESTS

Although this book will give you the practice and basic skills you need to take the GMAT, you might want to fine-tune your techniques by testing yourself with some real questions written by the test-writers, ETS. You can get a good idea of how a GMAT feels by using ETS's *PowerPrep Software*, which includes real GMAT questions presented in Computer Adaptive mode. Or, if you prefer a book, the same questions are available in ETS's *Official Guide to the GMAT*. Both of these are available in major bookstores by calling 800-982-6740, or online at www.gmat.org.

DISCLAIMER

At the time this book went to press, the information in it was current. The GMAT may change, however, which means that you should consult ETS's *GMAT Registration and Information* bulletin for the most up-to-date information. You can also get the latest information from ETS's website, www.ets.org, or our website, www.review.com.

GENERAL STRATEGY

HOW ADAPTIVE TESTING WORKS

Instead of subtracting the total number of incorrect answers from the total number of questions, computer-adaptive testing calculates your score progressively. Here's how it works: When you start each multiple-choice section of your GMAT, the computer knows nothing about you, so it estimates your score to be average, right in the middle of the scale. The first question you'll see in each section of the test is likewise a question of average difficulty, one that roughly 50 percent of test-takers answer correctly. As you proceed through the test the computer revises its assessment of you, both by giving you questions that are more or less difficult (depending on your answers), and by adjusting its estimate of your score up and down, until it has enough information to assign you a subscore for that section. Your subscores are then simply added and converted to your composite score.

HOW TO MAKE IT WORK FOR YOU

The computer weighs your performance on earlier questions more heavily than it does later ones. Early in the test, your score will move up and down (hopefully, up!) in large increments, but as you near the end, your score will change only by small amounts. With this in mind, you can use the structure of the test to your advantage.

Take a look at this diagram:

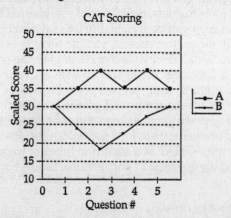

It shows the performance of two test-takers in the first five minutes of their respective tests. Test-taker A starts off well. She gets the first question right, and the computer's estimate of her score increases accordingly. The second question is more difficult, but she gets it right, too, and her score increases again. The third question is slightly more difficult than the previous two, and gives her some trouble. She gets it wrong, so her score drops. The fourth question, then, is a little easier, and she gets it right so her score goes back up. She misses the fifth question and the computer, at this point, estimates that her subscore is about 35.

Check out test-taker B. He misses the first two questions and his subscore plummets. He gets the third, fourth, and fifth questions right, but the computer estimates his subscore after five questions to be about five points lower than that of test-taker A's, even thought they've both missed two out of five. The moral of the story: Earlier questions are more important than later questions.

This means that you'll need to concentrate hardest on answering early questions correctly, even if this means spending more time on them than you'd like. You can make this time up by moving more quickly on later questions, when you'll affect your score less dramatically.

Remember that the questions are multiple choice, so the right answer is there, somewhere. But sometimes the challenge is not so much to identify the right answer, as it is to identify the four wrong ones. This brings us to our first technique, Process of Elimination (POE). By using POE you can improve your score on the GMAT.

POE

Let's say you're faced with a sentence-correction question you know contains an error, but you can't identify it. Since you can't skip the question, you'll have to guess, right? And if you guessed blindly, you'd have a 1 in 5 chance of getting it right. But let's say that by reading carefully through the answer choices, you can identify even one wrong answer and eliminate it. Then your chances of guessing correctly improve to 1 in 4. If you can eliminate two answers, your chances jump to 1 in 3. As you continue using process of elimination, you could even eliminate all the incorrect answers and get the question right, but at the very least you'll improve your chances of guessing correctly.

Every wrong answer is there for a reason. Oh yes, it's true. Every wrong answer on the GMAT was created in hopes of trapping a test-taker who solved the question by conventional means but made a careless but predictable error. There's always an answer waiting for these folks, appearing to be right when it isn't. By using POE to eliminate wrong answers instead of trying to divine the right one, you're less likely to fall into those traps.

The Best Answer

We'll say one more thing about POE and the four wrong answers. After you've eliminated four that definitely have something wrong with them, the answer you're left with may not fill you with joy. It may not seem right even after you've eliminated four that were less right. Don't fret—just go with it. You should know that ETS itself doesn't even use the term "right answer." They call it the "best answer," or "credited response." Keep this in mind as you're working through POE. Don't eliminate an answer simply because you don't like it. That answer may still be the best of the five.

Answer Every Question

You must answer every question on the GMAT, because you can't proceed to the next question without answering the one you're on. If you fail to answer every question in a section (even if the last few are guesses), you'll be penalized. How? The computer will take the score it calculated for you up to that point, and reduce it by roughly the percentage of the test that you've left unfinished. If you leave $\frac{1}{4}$ of the questions unanswered, the computer will reduce your score by 25 percent. Ouch! So do your best to record an answer for every question, even if you have to guess.

Watch the Clock

In the upper right corner of the computer screen, you will see the time that remains in your section. At first, time is displayed in hours and minutes (1:14). But when only five minutes remain, the display changes to minutes and seconds (4:59) and begins to flash. This is your signal to wrap it up. Quickly assess how close you are to the end, and accelerate your pace so you record an answer for every question.

Use Your Scratch Paper

Since all the questions appear on the computer screen, you will not have a test booklet in which to write. But the good news is you'll receive an unlimited supply of scratch paper. And to get the best results on the GMAT, you're going to have to use it.

For starters, you'll use your scratch paper to keep track of POE. It does no good to eliminate an answer choice if you keep reconsidering it. This means you need to *cross out* each answer choice as you eliminate it, but you can't cross them out on your computer screen. That's where your scratch paper comes in.

On the GMAT, each answer choice has a bubble next to it, but in this book we'll refer to them as (A), (B), (C), (D), and (E). Each time you see a question, get in the habit of immediately writing down *A, B, C, D,* and *E* on your scratch paper.

In fact, we recommend you set up a couple of sheets of your scratch paper for exactly this purpose:

A B C D E	A B C D E
A B C D E	A B C D E

This makes it less likely you'll lose your place or get confused. As you work through each question, you can eliminate those pesky wrong answer choices by crossing out its letter name on your paper. As you're crossing them out, it will become more evident which one is the best answer. When you're finished with the question, put an X through the box where your work and answers are. This will help you stay organized, calm, and efficient.

It's smart to try to simulate the test environment as best you can when you practice, so that on test day all your techniques and strategies will feel natural. As you practice, prepare your scratch paper in the way we showed you, and do all your calculations on it.

PART II

TEN STEPS TO THE GMAT

STEP 1

SENTENCE CORRECTION

Sentence correction questions comprise about one-third, or 14, of the questions on your GMAT Verbal section. According to ETS, these questions are "designed to measure your correct use of grammar, your ability to form clear and effective sentences and your capacity to choose the most appropriate words."

Doing well on this section has little to do with your ability to speak English fluently. Written English (with very strict rules of grammar) is what the GMAT is all about. See whether you can spot the grammatical flaw in the following sentence:

> Every daytrader finds the information to make their
> decisions in publications like *The Wall Street Journal*,
> *Bloomsberg*, and *The Financial Times*.

Don't see anything wrong with the sentence? That's what ETS is hoping. Although it sounds perfectly normal when spoken out loud, the sentence actually contains not one, but two grammatical errors.

On the GMAT, sentence correction questions consist of a sentence, part of which is underlined, followed by five answer choices that represent different ways of writing the underlined portion of the sentence. A single word, a short phrase, or the entire sentence may be underlined. The first answer choice, (A), always repeats the underlined portion of the original sentence with no changes. Answer choices (B), (C), (D), and (E) will be alternate ways of expressing the same idea.

Most people approach sentence correction questions in the wrong way. The average test-taker, for example, reads the sentence, spots what he or she thinks is the error in the underlined portion, mentally fixes the sentence, and chooses the answer choice that comes closest to what sounds right to him or her. There are a couple of problems with this approach. One, ETS deliberately makes the errors hard to spot, and two, ETS is *very* good at writing incorrect answer choices.

Some incorrect answer choices repeat a grammatical error in the original sentence, rewriting another part of the sentence that didn't originally contain an error. Others fix the error of the original sentence but introduce a new error. To avoid falling into the traps ETS sets for you on sentence correction, follow our approach.

THE THREE-STEP APPROACH

The key to cracking sentence correction questions is to know what types of grammatical errors ETS likes to test most. This along with a systematic use of Process of Elimination will help you do well on this section. The three-step approach you'll use is listed below:

Let's take a look at a sentence correction question and try out the three-step approach.

> In response to rising health care costs, the insurance company instituted a new policy <u>which requires patients to receive</u> a referral from a primary care physician before seeing a specialist.
>
> ○ which requires patients to receive
> ○ that requires patients to receive
> ○ which requires patients receive
> ○ which requires that patients are receiving
> ○ that requires patients receive

Step 1: Read the Question and Identify the Error.

Read the entire sentence closely, making sure you understand the context of the underlined portion. Let's assume you spot the error right away: the incorrect use of *which*. You're ready for Step Two.

Step 2: Eliminate All Answer Choices Containing That Error.

Since you have spotted the error, you can go through the answer choices (write *A, B, C, D, E* on your scratch paper) and eliminate all the ones that begin with *which*. That gets rid of answer choices (A), (C), and (D).

Step 3: Look for Grammar Errors in the Remaining Answer Choices and Eliminate Them.

Compare answer choices (B) and (E). The only difference is that (B) says *to receive* and (E) just says *receive*. If you know that the verb *require* is always followed by an infinitive, you know that (E) *that requires patients receive* is incorrect. Eliminate it, and you're left with (B), which is the correct answer.

PLAN B

Perhaps you don't remember the difference between *that* and *which*. Don't worry—we'll review this, along with several other common constructions and idioms, later in this chapter. But let's imagine for a moment that, even after poring over all the material in this chapter, you see a sentence correction question and cannot identify the error. There are two possible reasons for this. The error may be very difficult to identify, or the sentence may not contain an error at all.

The best strategy here is to go directly to the answer choices and look for a grammatical error in each one. Chances are, you'll be able to eliminate at least three of them. Then compare the two that remain—the difference between them should be that one contains the error that the sentence is testing. Determine which one is incorrect and eliminate it.

Don't Overcorrect

Remember that the sentence may be correct as it is written. Answer choice (A) always repeats the underlined portion of the sentence exactly as it appears in the original sentence, and it *will* be correct some of the time. If you've gone through Step One and cannot spot the error, go straight to the answer choices and start eliminating them as we advised in Plan B. You may find that you're left with the original sentence.

Be careful, too, of what sounds good. The GMAT tests the strict rules of written grammar, so relying on your ear to lead you to the correct answer is not a good strategy.

More on Process of Elimination

Take another look at the answer choices for the sentence about the insurance company. Notice that three of the answer choices begin with *which* and the other two begin with *that*. We call this a 2/3 Split, and this pattern can clue you in to the grammar error that the sentence is testing. In this case, if you can determine whether *which* or *that* is correct, you can eliminate that entire set of answer choices.

Six Commonly Tested Errors

You now have an overview of sentence correction problems and the basic techniques for approaching them. Now we'll list six commonly tested errors and teach you how to spot and fix each one.

Misplaced Modifier

Rule: A descriptive word or phrase should immediately follow the thing that it modifies.

How to spot it: Two phrases are separated by a comma and one or both of them are underlined.

How to fix it: Choose an answer choice that puts the modifying phrase and the object it's modifying right next to each other (separated by a comma).

Example:

> A dairy cow known for its gentle temperament, <u>the milk of the Jersey is high in fat content and suitable for either drinking or processing</u>.

- ○ the milk of the Jersey is high in fat content and suitable for either drinking or processing
- ○ the milk of the Jersey is high in fat content, suited for either drinking or processing
- ○ the Jersey gives milk that is high in fat content and suitable for either drinking or processing
- ○ the milk of the Jersey is high in fat content and suitable either to drink or to process
- ○ the Jersey gives milk that is high in fat content, suitable for either drinking or processing

Step 1: Read the Question and Identify the Error. Since the underlined portion of the sentence comes directly after a comma, there is a good chance that the error here is a misplaced modifier. What does the modifying phrase, *A dairy cow known for its gentle temperament*, modify—the cow or the milk? It should modify the cow, but as the sentence is written, the modifying phrase modifies the milk.

Step 2: Eliminate All Answer Choices Containing That Error. Since you've identified the error, you can now eliminate all the answer choices in the 2/3 split that contain the same error—(A), (B), and (D)—and you're down to two answer choices.

Step 3: Look for Grammar Errors in the Remaining Answer Choices and Eliminate Them. Compare answer choices (C) and (E)—what's the difference between them? Choice (C) contains the word *and*, while choice (E) simply has a comma. Which is right? Well, answer choice (E), in which the *and* is replaced with a comma, contains the modifying phrase *suitable for either drinking or processing*. This phrase incorrectly modifies *fat content*, which precedes it. Answer choice (E) is grammatically incorrect, so eliminate it.

Pronouns

Rule: A pronoun must clearly refer to a noun, and must agree with that noun in gender and quantity.

How to spot it: A pronoun is in the underlined portion of the sentence.

How to fix it: Identify the pronoun and the noun it replaces. Change the pronoun so that it agrees with the noun.

Example:

> The average Olympic athlete begins training at the age of 10, although <u>they may not compete</u> for several more years.
>
> O   they may not compete
> O   they might not compete
> O   she may not compete
> O   it does not compete
> O   competition is not their goal

Step 1: Read the Sentence and Identify the Error. The error must be in either the pronoun or verb use, since that's pretty much all the underlined portion of the sentence contains. The way to determine whether *they* is the correct pronoun is to try to match it with the noun it modifies, in this case, *athlete*. *Athlete* is singular, so you need a singular pronoun (not a plural one, like *they*) such as he or she (*it* cannot refer to people).

If you do not immediately know that the pronoun is incorrect, you can look through the answer choices and start eliminating those that definitely contain an error. But when you see a pronoun in the underlined portion of the sentence, you should always check it—pronoun errors are very common on the GMAT.

Step 2: Eliminate All Answer Choices Containing That Error. The error is that the sentence contains a singular noun and a plural pronoun. Eliminate answer choices (A), (B), and (E) because all the pronouns in these choices are plural.

Step 3: Look for Grammar Errors in the Remaining Answer Choices and Eliminate Them. Compare answer choices (C) and (D). You know that *it* cannot refer to people, so eliminate choice (D). Answer choice (C) is the answer.

Subject/Verb Agreement

Rule: A subject must always agree with its verb.

How to spot it: Typically, in a sentence with a subject/verb error, ETS places the subject and verb as far away from each other as possible.

How to fix it: Identify the subject and verb of the sentence or phrase, and make sure they agree in number.

Example:

> The members of the newest wave of world-class chefs have created a cuisine characterized not only by excellence but also eclecticism: the traditional techniques of French cuisine form a foundation to which is added Latin American, Asian, and African elements.

- ○ to which is added Latin American, Asian, and African elements
- ○ added to which is Latin American, Asian, and African elements
- ○ to which Latin American, Asian, and African elements are added
- ○ with Latin American, Asian, and African elements being added to it
- ○ and, in addition, Latin American, Asian, and African elements are added

Step 1: Read the Sentence and Identify the Error. Since there is a verb in the underlined portion, you should suspect subject/verb agreement as the possible source of error. As you can see, the verb *is added* is singular and doesn't agree with the noun it modifies, in this case, *elements* which is plural. So what you need is the plural verb *are added*.

Step 2: Eliminate All Answer Choices Containing That Error. Eliminating the singular verbs gets rid of choices (A) and (B).

Step 3: Look for Grammar Errors in the Remaining Answer Choices and Eliminate Them. Nothing appears to be wrong with answer choice (C). It has the plural verb *are added* and although it's a modifying phrase, it modifies the word immediately before it, *foundation*. Choice (D), on the other hand, contains the word *being*, which is not an acceptable way to conjugate a verb (the *ing* ending goes on the main verb, not the helping verb). Therefore, choice (D) is incorrect. Keep your eye out for the word *being*; ETS loves to use it, but it is almost always used incorrectly. Answer choice (E) is redundant, *and . . . in addition . . . added*, and should be eliminated. Choice (C) is the best answer.

Another note on subject/verb agreement: Words such as *none, no one,* and *every* are singular, and should be followed by a singular verb. Examples:

No one who lives here is at home.

None of the executives hired last year is still employed here.

Every burglary in the neighborhood is the work of a well-known jewel thief.

Parallel Construction

Rule: Items in a list or items that are being compared, must all contain the same parts of speech, and must *look* the same.

How to spot it: If the sentence contains a list or comparison, you should probably look for a parallel construction error.

How to fix it: Find the list or comparison in the nonunderlined portion of the sentence. Change the nonmatching member of the list or comparison so that it matches the other members.

Example:

> General contracting firms are investigating changes in construction techniques that would permit contractors to reduce the time required to complete construction of a building, <u>decrease the amount of raw material needed during construction, and to avoid changes that require contractors that revise blueprints</u> and redraft working plans.

- ○ decrease the amount of raw material needed during construction, and to avoid changes that require contractors that revise blueprints
- ○ decrease the amount of raw material needed during construction, and avoiding changes that require contractors revising blueprints
- ○ to decrease the amount of raw material needed during construction, and avoiding changes that require contractors to revise blueprints
- ○ to decrease the amount raw material needed during construction, avoiding changes that require contractors that revise blueprints
- ○ to decrease the amount of raw material needed during construction, and to avoid changes that require contractors to revise blueprints

Step 1: Read the Sentence and Identify the Error. You have both *decrease* and *to avoid* in the underlined portion. These words are not parallel. Furthermore, the verb *require* must be followed by an infinitive, in this case, *to revise*.

Step 2: Eliminate All Answer Choices Containing That Error. Your list starts with *to reduce* in the nonunderlined portion. When you have a list of infinitives like this one, the initial *to* can cover all the verbs listed. So a good answer choice would read *decrease . . . and avoid* or *to decrease . . . and to avoid*. You'll need to check each answer choice very carefully to find reasons to eliminate it. Get rid of choice (A), *decrease . . . and to* *avoid;* choice (B), *decrease . . . and avoiding;* and choice (C), *to decrease . . . and avoiding,* because none of these is parallel.

Step 3: Look for Grammar Errors in the Remaining Answer Choices and Eliminate Them. Answer choice (D) reads *to decrease . . . , avoiding* making the final phrase a modifier. *Avoiding changes* does not modify *construction,* so eliminate it. Choice (E) reads *to decrease . . . and to avoid,* which is an acceptable way to complete this list.

That's an example of a parallel construction containing a list. Let's look at one that contains a comparison.

Example:

> The rules of rugby are more liberal <u>than soccer</u>.
>
> ○   than soccer
> ○   as soccer
> ○   as those of soccer
> ○   than those of soccer
> ○   than soccer is

Step 1: Read the Sentence and Identify the Error. The word *than* is underlined, so you're dealing with a parallel construction that centers on a comparison. Identify what you're comparing (the rules of rugby and the rules of soccer) and look for an answer choice that makes the comparison clear. The error here is that the way the sentence currently reads, you're comparing "rules" to "soccer."

Step 2: Eliminate All Answer Choices Containing That Error. Eliminate answer choices (A), (B), and (E), because they all compare "rules" to "soccer."

Step 3: Look for Grammar Errors in the Remaining Answer Choices and Eliminate Them. Choices (C) and (D) differ only in that choice (C) contains *as* and choice (D) contains *than.* The correct idiom is *more . . . than.* Choice (D) is the best answer.

Verb Tense

Simple past, present perfect, and past perfect are three verb tenses most commonly tested on the GMAT. You do not need to worry about what they're called; focus on learning how to identify their correct usage.

Rule:

Use the	When an action started in the past and . . .	
Simple Past	Has ceased to occur	Alex looked puzzled when you told him the news.
Present Perfect	Continues to the present	As long as I have known him, Alex has looked puzzled in meetings.
Past Perfect	Was completed before some other past action began.	Alex had always looked puzzled in meeting until he got a new boss.

How to spot it: The sentence contains an action, or it contains a series of actions occurring at different times.

How to fix it: Identify the sequence of events in the sentence. Use the table above to determine the correct verb tense.

Example:

Some epidemiologists believe that the Ebola virus <u>has originated from an animal host in a less populated region of Africa and has flourished in areas</u> where there is more frequent contact between humans and wild animals.

- ○ has originated from an animal host in a less populated region of Africa and has flourished in areas
- ○ originated from an animal host in a less populated region of Africa and has flourished in areas
- ○ has originated from an animal host in a less populated region of Africa and had flourished in areas
- ○ originated from an animal host in a less populated region of Africa and had flourished in areas
- ○ originated from an animal host in a less populated region of Africa and flourished in areas

Step 1: Read the Sentence and Identify the Error. The series of events (*has originated . . . has flourished*) in the underlined portion points to a verb tense error. The first event is one that can occur only once (something can *originate* only once) and thus calls for the simple past, *originated*. The second event began in the past and continues into the present, so *has flourished* is correct.

Step 2: Eliminate All Answer Choices Containing That Error. The 2/3 split with *originated/has originated* allows you to eliminate choices (A) and (C).

Step 3: Look for Grammar Errors in the Remaining Answer Choices and Eliminate Them. Of the remaining answer choices, only choice (B) contains the correct tense *has flourished*.

Idioms and Style

The last category of grammar errors ETS likes to test is actually a list of grammatical constructions called idioms. There is no strict rule governing the use of idioms; there is simply a list of words and phrases you'll need to memorize. The good news is that once you learn to recognize them, you'll always know how to fix them. A list of the 50 most common idiomatic phrases and constructions is located at the end of this chapter (page 26).

Let's wrap up this chapter with some pointers on style.

Occasionally, you'll be left with two answer choices that differ only in style. In this case, eliminate the answer choice that is redundant, wordier, or written in the passive voice.

Example:

> After Al Gore spent weeks trying to resuscitate his dying campaign, <u>yielding the nomination to Bill Bradley was chosen by Gore</u> rather than to face further humiliation and bankruptcy.

- ○ yielding the nomination to Bill Bradley was chosen by Gore
- ○ to yield the nomination to Bill Bradley was chosen by Gore
- ○ Gore chose to yield the nomination to Bill Bradley
- ○ Gore chose yielding the nomination to Bill Bradley
- ○ yielding the nomination to Bill Bradley was chosen by Gore

Step 1: Read the Sentence and Identify the Error. Did you see that the error was one of parallel construction; *yielding . . . rather than face?* Good.

Step 2: Eliminate All Answer Choices Containing That Error. This gets rid of choices (A), (D), and (E).

Step 3: Look for Grammar Errors in the Remaining Answer Choices and Eliminate Them. Answer choices (B) and (C) say the same thing, and both are grammatically correct, but choice (B) is written in passive voice. So although there is nothing technically wrong with (B), choice (C) is a better answer.

Idioms

Here are 50 of the most frequently tested idiomatic constructions on the GMAT:

1. Where *or* when vs. that *or* in which

Do not use *where* or *when* instead of *in which* or *that*. These words are most commonly misused in this way:

INCORRECT:

The talk show host agitated the guests to the point *where* they were throwing chairs at each other.

I look back fondly on the 1983 County Fair, *when* I won the prize for biggest watermelon.

CORRECT:

The talk show host agitated the guests to the point *that* they were throwing chairs at each other.

I look back fondly on the 1983 County Fair, at *which* I won the prize for biggest watermelon.

Use *where* only when you're referring to an actual location.

That desk is *where* I spend countless hours working at my thankless job.

Use *when* only to denote a moment in time.

I'll go out with you *when* the clock strikes thirteen, and not a moment sooner.

2. Who vs. whom

Who is a subject or direct object, and *whom* is an indirect object.

Who left the door open?

I can't wait to see *whom* she'll bring to dinner this time.

If you tend to confuse these two, try replacing *who* or *whom* with *he* or *him*. If the sentence or clause should use *he*, use *who*; if the sentence calls for *him*, use *whom*.

> He left the door open. (Use *who*.)

> ... she'll bring him to dinner this time. (Use *whom*.)

3. Not only . . . but also

> You are *not only* clever, but you are *also* charming.

4. Not so . . . as

> I am *not so* foolish *as* to fall for that a third time.

5. Not . . . but

> The basketball player is *not* tall, *but* he is fast.

6. Either . . . or

> I'll take *either* a BMW *or* a Lexus; I'm not particular.

7. Neither . . . nor

> I will eat *neither* tomatoes *nor* brussel sprouts; they smell funny.

8. Both . . . and

> You should admit you're afraid of *both* clowns *and* elephants.

9. More . . . than

> That weightlifter has *more* muscle in his head *than* he has brains.

10. Comparatives

Two separate sets of words are used when making comparisons. Use the first set when you are comparing only two things. Use the second set when you are comparing three or more things.

Only two things	Three or more things
More	Most
–er	–est
Between	Among

Only two things:

> Between cake and ice cream, I like ice cream *more*.

Three or more things:

> Among the three sisters, Cinderella was the *most* beautiful.

11. The more . . . the –er

The *more* you eat, the fatter you get.

12. Just as . . . so too

Just as I have found my cell phone indispensable, *so* you will *too*.

13. As . . . as

Washing my car in the winter is not *as* easy *as* it is in the summer.

14. Quantity words

Quantity words are tested on the GMAT because they are commonly confused. If you can physically count the things you're referring to, use the words in the first column. If you can't, use the words in the second column.

Can be counted	Cannot be counted
Many	Much
Number	Amount
Fewer	Less

Can be counted:

Give a child as *many* hugs as you can.

No one can drink that *number* of cocktails without becoming drunk.

Cannot be counted:

Give a child as *much* love as you can.

No one can drink that *amount* of whisky without becoming drunk.

15. The number of vs. A number of

When you use *the number of* you should use a singular verb (*the number* is single).

The number of excuses grows every time he tells the story.

But when you use *a number of*, use a plural verb, as *a number* of something is a multitude.

A number of survivors of the plane crash swam to shore.

16. The same . . . as

Although she looks much older, Faye Dunaway is *the same* age *as* my mother.

17. Different from

You are no *different from* me; we both want success.

18. Superior . . . to

"ER" is a *superior* television show *to* "Chicago Hope."

19. Distinguish . . . from

Dazed by the battle, the soldier could no longer *distinguish* friend *from* enemy.

20. Associate with

My dad says I can no longer *associate with* you.

21. Between . . . and

April found herself choosing *between* the devil *and* the deep blue sea.

22. Contrast . . . with

If you *contrast* one politician's ethics *with* another's, you will find no difference.

23. Responsibility to

It is my *responsibility to* feed the parakeet.

24. Responsible for

I am *responsible for* feeding the parakeet.

25. Require . . . to

Sheep herding *requires* a shepherd *to* stay with his flock at all times.

26. Forbid . . . to

I *forbid* you *to* interrupt me again.

27. Prohibit . . . from

I can physically *prohibit* you *from* interrupting me again.

28. Worry about

She *worried about* where they would hide the loot.

29. Permit to

Convicted felons are not *permitted to* vote.

30. Try to

Please *try to* chew with your mouth closed at the awards dinner tonight.

31. Ability . . . to

He has an *ability to* turn around a failing business.

32. Believe . . . to be

I no longer *believe* the tooth fairy *to be* real.

33. Consider

Many *consider* Henry Kissinger the greatest statesman of the twentieth century.

34. Estimate ... to be

The sideshow barker *estimated* Henry *to be* a fool.

35. Define ... as

Republicans *define* welfare abuse *as* the primary evil in America.

36. Regard ... as

Shakespeare is *regarded as* the greatest playwright of all time.

37. Think of ... as

She *thinks of* me *as* just a friend.

38. See ... as

My father *sees* a large investment portfolio *as* a sign of success.

39. Native

Native requires two different constructions: one when it's a noun, and a different one when it's used as an adjective.

NOUN: *NATIVE* ... *OF*

Not surprisingly, Donald Trump is a *native of* New York City.

ADJECTIVE: *NATIVE* ... *TO*

Okra is *native to* Africa.

40. That vs. which

This is perhaps the most commonly misused construction in English. *That* and *which* are both used to introduce modifiers. The key is to determine whether the modifying information is required or extraneous. If it is required, use *that*.

THAT:

The lawnmower *that* you came to fix is in the garage.

You need the *that you came to fix* so we know which lawnmower we're talking about.

WHICH:

The lawnmower, *which* is in the garage, is broken beyond repair.

The sentence is about the lawnmower and its state of disrepair. The information about where it is located (*which is in the garage*) is extraneous.

41. As vs. like

A good rule of thumb for the word *like* is to avoid it if another word or phrase will work. *As* is used to compare noun/verb combinations. *Like* is used when comparing only nouns.

> He does not bathe every day, *as* I do.

> That car is just *like* one my father had.

42. Like vs. such as

Again, don't use *like* if another word or phrase will do. Use *such as* when you mean *for example,* and use *like* when you mean *similar to.*

> Many of the top designers, *such as* Ralph Lauren and Donna Karan, have less expensive lines as well.

> Why must you act *like* a four-year-old?

43. From . . . to

> Route 66 is a highway that runs *from* Chicago *to* Los Angeles.

44. Attribute . . . to

> Many theories in contemporary psychology are *attributed to* Freud.

45. Credit . . . with

> Benjamin Franklin is *credited with* the invention of the U.S. postal system.

46. Each vs. all *or* both

Use *each* when you want to emphasize that items are separate. Use *both* or *all* when you want to emphasize that items are together or similar.

> *Each* of the schools he applied to had its own strengths.

> *Both* of the programs were highly regarded.

> *All* of the schools offer financial assistance.

47. So . . . that

> She was *so* blunt *that* many considered her rude.

48. So . . . as to be

> Joe is *so* smart *as to be* intimidating.

49. Hypothesis that

Circulating on the Internet is a *hypothesis that* the aluminum in soda cans causes Alzheimer's disease.

50. Target . . . at

Many cigarette companies *target* their advertising *at* children.

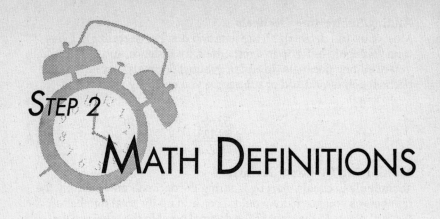

STEP 2
MATH DEFINITIONS

Welcome back to ninth grade! The math on the GMAT, while sometimes presented in a potentially confusing way, does not rely on your ability to perform any advanced mathematical operations. Once you understand what each problem is asking, you will be doing relatively simple, straightforward calculations, such as multiplying, converting fractions to decimals, factoring, and solving for x.

MATHEMATICAL DEFINITIONS AND THE BASICS

We know it's probably been a while since you did ninth grade math, so let's start off with a review of some of the vocabulary and mathematical operations you'll encounter on the GMAT.

Coefficient

The number 3 in front of the variable in an expression like $3xy$ is called the **coefficient**.

Consecutive

Consecutive describes integers listed in ascending order, which are separated by the same interval. The numbers 1, 2, 3, 4 are consecutive integers, and the numbers 2, 4, 6, 8 are consecutive even integers.

Decimals

Like fractions, **decimals** are a way of expressing parts of a whole. When given the option of working with fractions or decimals, fractions tend to be simpler and safer, but you'll also need to be comfortable adding, subtracting, multiplying, and dividing decimal expressions.

Adding/Subtracting Decimals

Most of us add decimals all the time and don't even realize it. Every time you figure out a tip in a restaurant, for instance, and pay your bill, you're adding decimals. To add or subtract decimals, just line up the decimal points, and add or subtract as you normally would.

Example:

$$
\begin{array}{r}
50.650 \\
+\ 28.123 \\
\hline
78.773
\end{array}
$$

Multiplying/Dividing Decimals

To multiply decimals, start by ignoring the decimals and multiply the numbers as you normally would. Then add up the total number of decimal places to the right of the decimal point in the numbers you multiplied, and put the decimal point the same number of digits over from the right, in your product.

Example:

$$
\begin{array}{r}
5.2 \\
\times\ 2.5 \\
\hline
260 \\
1040 \\
\hline
1300
\end{array}
$$

There is one place to the right of each of the original multiples, so move the decimal point over two from the right, in the answer, to get 13.00.

Difference

The result of subtraction is called the **difference**.

Digit *are the numbers on a telephone*

The **digits** are 0, 1, 2, 3, 4, 5, 6, 7, 8, and 9—the numbers you see on a telephone. GMAT math problems might ask you either to count digits or supply a missing digit. Try counting the digits in 2654.189. There are seven.

Distinct

Distinct is simply a mathematical way of saying "different." So when you are asked to count the distinct prime factors of 12, you would answer that there are two—2 and 3. Even though 12 = 2 × 2 × 3, you can only count 2 once.

Dividend

The number you are dividing another number *into* is the **dividend**.

Divisible

When a number can be divided evenly by another number, it is said to be **divisible** by that number. So 6 is divisible by 3, but is not divisible by 4. The GMAT, however, is more likely to ask you whether 728 is divisible by 4. (Yes, it is.)

Some rules to help you check quickly for divisibility.

A # IS DIVISIBLE BY	IF
2	It ends in 0, 2, 4, 6, or 8.
3	Adding its digits yields a number divisible by 3.
4	The last two digits, considered as a number, are divisible by 4. Example: Take 728. The last two digits form the number 28, which is divisible by 4.
5	It ends in 5 or 0.
6	It is divisible by both 2 and 3.
7	There is no easy test for divisibility by 7, but you won't be asked about it, either.
8	There is no easy test, but in a pinch, you can divide by 2 and check whether or not the resulting number is divisible by 4.
9	Adding its digits results in a number that's a multiple of 9.

Even/Odd Numbers

An **even** number is one that can be divided evenly by 2. Even numbers are whole and they end in 2, 4, 6, 8, or 0. The number zero (0) is considered even.

An **odd** number is a whole number that, when divided by two, yields a remainder of 1. Odd numbers end in 1, 3, 5, 7, or 9.

Exponent

An **exponent** simply tells you to "multiply this number x times." So $2^3 = 2 \times 2 \times 2$, or 8. The number you multiply is called the **base**, and the little superscript number that tells you how many times to multiply the base is called an exponent or a **power**. So in 3^2, 3 is the base and 2 is the power.

HERE ARE SOME MORE RULES ABOUT EXPONENTS:

Any number to the 1 power is itself: $5^1 = 5$

Any number to the 0 power is 1: $5^0 = 1$

Any positive number greater than 1, raised to a power greater than 1 becomes larger. For example, $3^2 = 9$.

Any negative number raised to an even power becomes positive, but any negative number raised to an odd power stays negative. So $-3^4 = 81$, but $-3^3 = -27$.

Any fraction between 0 and 1 that's raised to a power greater than 1 gets smaller. For example,

$$\left(\frac{1}{2}\right)^2 = \frac{1}{4}.$$

Negative exponents—when you see a negative exponent, just turn the base into a fraction by

putting a 1 over it and proceed as you would with a nonnegative exponent. So $3^{-2} = \left(\frac{1}{3}\right)^2 = \frac{1}{9}$.

Fractional Exponents
Fractional exponents are pretty much just another way of writing square roots. See *Square Roots* for more information.

Adding and Subtracting Exponents
To add and subtract exponents, both the base and the power must be the same. If they are, just add or subtract as you normally would. So $3x^2 5x^2 = 8x^2$.

Multiplying and Dividing Exponents
When multiplying or dividing exponents, make sure that the bases are the same. To multiply, add the exponents and multiply the coefficients, and to divide, subtract the exponents and divide the coefficients.

Example:

$$3x^2 \times 5x^3 = 15x^5 \quad \text{and} \quad \frac{15x^6}{3x^2} = 5x^4$$

Factors

Factors are numbers that can be divided into another number without leaving a remainder. For example, the numbers 1, 2, 3, 4, 6, and 12 are the factors of 12.

Fractions

A **fraction** is the most basic expression of parts of a whole. For example, if a whole pizza has 8 slices and James eats 3, he has eaten $\frac{3}{8}$ of the pizza.

Numerator/Denominator

The top number in a fraction is called the **numerator**, and the bottom number is called the **denominator**.

Reducing Fractions

On the GMAT fractions are expressed in their most reduced form. This means that you'll have to simplify your answers, for instance, by reducing fractions. To reduce a fraction, simply find a number that's a factor of both its numerator and denominator, and factor it out, like this:

$$\frac{35}{49} = \frac{5 \times 7}{7 \times 7} = \frac{5}{7} \times \frac{7}{7} = \frac{5}{7} \times 1 = \frac{5}{7}$$

Reducing a fraction makes it easier to work with, which makes it less likely that you'll commit an error. Common factors to start with when you're reducing are 2, 3, and 5.

Adding/Subtracting Fractions

If you need to add or subtract two fractions that have the same denominator, simply add or subtract their numerators, like this:

$$\frac{3}{4} + \frac{1}{4} = \frac{4}{4}, \text{ or } 1$$

If the numbers in the denominators are different, this operation will involve a couple of extra steps. The **Bowtie** is a simple way of adding and subtracting fractions like these:

$$\frac{5}{8} + \frac{3}{5}$$

To use the bowtie method, first multiply straight across the bottom of the fraction to find a common denominator. Then multiply top to bottom, top to bottom, like a bowtie. Finally, add or subtract to find the numerator.

$$\frac{5}{8} + \frac{3}{5} = \overset{25}{\underset{24}{\frac{5}{8} \diagdown\!\!\!\!\times\!\!\!\!\diagup \frac{3}{5}}} = \frac{25+24}{8\times5} = \frac{49}{40}$$

Multiplying and Dividing Fractions

When multiplying two or more fractions, just multiply their numerators, and then their denominators.

$$\frac{2}{5} \times \frac{3}{4} = \frac{2\times3}{5\times4} = \frac{6}{20} = \frac{3}{10}$$

Dividing fractions works a lot like multiplying fractions, with one important extra step. To divide fractions, multiply the first by the **reciprocal** of the second. So flip the second fraction and multiply in the regular way.

$$\frac{2}{5} \div \frac{3}{4} = \frac{2}{5} \times \frac{4}{3} = \frac{2\times4}{5\times3} = \frac{8}{15}$$

Cross-Multiplication

To solve an equation that contains two fractions containing variables *when they're equal to each other*, you can simply cross multiply, or multiply the top of each fraction by the bottom of the other.

For example:

$$\frac{3x}{4} = \frac{3}{2}$$

Cross-multiply the top of the first fraction by the bottom of the second, and vice versa.

$$\frac{3x}{4} = \frac{3}{2}$$
$$= (3x)(2) = (3)(4)$$
$$= 6x = 12$$
$$x = 12$$

Integer

An **integer** is any whole number, positive, negative, or zero. So –3, 100, and 0 are all integers.

Multiple

The result of multiplying any number by any other number is called a **multiple**. The numbers 8, 16, and 424 are all multiples of 4.

Order of Operations

Order of operations refers to just what it sounds like: the order in which mathematical operations are to be performed. There's a phrase that will help you remember all the operations in their proper order: Please Excuse My Dear Aunt Sally. It stands for Parentheses, Exponents, Multiplication, Division, Addition, and Subtraction. Start with the parentheses and work your way from inside to outside. Next come exponents, and then do multiplication and division, from left to right. Last, do any remaining addition and subtraction; again, from left to right.

For example:

$$2 + 10 \times 6$$

If you follow the order of operations and work multiplication before addition, you get

$$2 + (10 \times 6)$$

$$2 + (60)$$

You'll arrive at the correct answer, 62.

If you simply worked from left to right, you'd get

$$(2 + 10) \times 6$$

$$12 \times 6$$

which is equal to 72; that's incorrect.

Positive/Negative Numbers

A <u>**positive number** is any number greater than 0</u>. So $\frac{1}{4}$ is a positive number, as is 5,000, but 0 is not.

Any number that's less than 0 is a **negative number**. The number <u>–15 is negative</u>. Zero is not.

Prime Numbers

Prime numbers have exactly two distinct factors: 1 and themselves. For example, 13 is prime because its only factors are 1 and 13. The number 1 is not prime; it has only one distinct factor.

Product

The result of multiplication is called the **product**.

Quotient
The result of division is called the **quotient**.

Reciprocal
The inverse of a number or fraction is the **reciprocal**. For example, the reciprocal of $\frac{5}{8}$ is $\frac{8}{5}$.

Remainder
The **remainder** is the number that's left over after division. The remainder when you divide 35 by 8 is 3.

Square Root
Remember this magical symbol: $\sqrt{}$? It indicates the **square root** of a number. So $\sqrt{16} = 4$ or -4, because both $(4)^2$ and $(-4)^2 = 16$.

You cannot add square roots unless they have a common root (the number of term under the square root sign). So $\sqrt{2} + \sqrt{2} = 2\sqrt{2}$. But $\sqrt{2} + \sqrt{3}$ is not equal to $\sqrt{5}$. To multiply or divide square roots, just treat them as regular integers: $\sqrt{6} \times \sqrt{3} = \sqrt{18}$, or $3\sqrt{2}$. Basically, they're subject to the same rules as exponents. In fact, a square root is an exponent: $x^{\frac{1}{2}}$ is just $\sqrt{x}$.

Sum
The result of addition is called the **sum**.

Whole Number
A **whole number** is a number that does not have any fractional parts. The number 2 is a whole number, but 2.5 is not.

Zero
Zero is an integer, it's neither positive or negative, and it's even. Multiplying by 0 always gives you a product of 0, and dividing by zero is impossible.

STEP 3

ARGUMENTS

Consider the statement, "Buy American cars, because they're better. They're made by American workers." The author of the statement is trying to convince you of something, right? His point is that you should buy an American car, and the reason he gives in support of this point is that American cars are better because Americans make them. To refute his argument, you could give an example of a better way of determining what makes a car superior, or you could present a case in which a product made by American workers is inferior.

On the GMAT, statements like the one above are followed by a question and five answer choices. ETS calls this type of question "critical reasoning," but we call it an argument. Why? Well, each problem contains a paragraph, within which the author states a point and argues it with facts.

One-third of your GMAT Verbal section will be arguments, which means you'll see about 14 of them. Go ahead and take a closer look at the argument below:

> Although fresh oats and corn are the most
> nutritious foods for cattle, historically, cattle
> ranchers have minimized purchases of these
> grains in order to minimize costs due to spoilage.
> This year, however, fresh oats and corn have
> become the best-selling foods for cattle—a clear
> sign that cattle ranchers are putting nutrition
> ahead of concerns about costs due to spoilage.

Which of the following, if true, most seriously weakens the argument above?

- ○ Last year, processed cattle feed outsold fresh oats and corn by a wide margin.

- ○ No cattle ranchers have reported in surveys that they are attempting to purchase more nutritious fodder for their herds.

- ○ Higher temperatures and increased rain this year have led to quicker spoilage of fresh oats and corn that in previous years, when fresh oats and corn sold poorly to cattle ranchers.

- ○ Because of crop failures, all types of cattle fodder—including fresh oats and corn, processed cattle feed, and frozen nutritional supplements—were more expensive this year than in previous years.

- ○ Because of agricultural innovations, fresh oats and corn spoil much less quickly than in previous years, while the purchase price for such fodder has remained constant.

If you're like most people, you raced through the argument, glanced at the question, and went straight to the answer choices. You may have even jumped back and forth several times from the passage to the answer choices, wasting time, and perhaps not even ending up with the best answer. There's a better way to tackle these argument problems.

THE FOUR-STEP APPROACH

It doesn't do much good to read the argument before you know what you're looking for. In our Four-Step approach, you read the question first so you know what sorts of things to look for. You start by answering the questions in your own words, and by aggressively using POE to eliminate wrong answer choices. To introduce you to the Four-Step approach, we'll work through the argument above together.

Step 1: Read the Question

Yes, that's right. Skip over the argument entirely and go straight to the question. Why? Because reading the question will tell you what to look for in the passage. Once you know that, you can read through the argument with a purpose, and you'll get more out of the argument by knowing what you're looking for. Here's the question again:

Which of the following, if true, most seriously
weakens the argument above?

Now we know what we're looking for—a way to weaken the
author's argument. We might find that the author has come to a
conclusion that he does not support with facts, or we might determine
that, in constructing his argument, the author has neglected to rule out
other possible causes or outcomes. He may have included information
in the conclusion that's unsupported or even unmentioned in the body
of the argument. We may find his reasoning circular, overly general,
hyperbolic, or in some other way illogical. So when we read the
argument, we'll look for weak spots to attack—places where the
reasoning of the argument is flawed. That's our next step.

Step 2: Break It Down

To break down an argument, we'll first need to identify the author's
main idea, or point, and then the reasons he cites to support that point.
The author's point, as we mentioned above, is what he's trying to
convince you of—it's the whole reason why he wrote the argument. If
you have trouble determining the point, try asking yourself, "What's he
trying to say? If he were writing a TV commercial, what would he be
selling? If he were a politician, what would he be advocating?" The
answer to any one of these questions is the author's point.

You'll also need to take note of the facts or reasons the author uses
in supporting his point. Does he cite a survey? Outline a chain of cause
and effect? Refer to authorities, publications, or popular opinion? Does
he bring up historical evidence? We'll call each piece of evidence the
author uses to support his argument a *premise*.

If you're having trouble locating the premises in the argument, try
using this simple test: State the conclusion, and then ask yourself,
"Why?" The information that answers the question "why?" are the
author's premises.

As you read, also keep an eye out for flaws or weaknesses, as we
discussed above. Okay, here's the argument again:

> *Although fresh oats and corn are the most
> nutritious foods for cattle, historically, cattle
> ranchers have minimized purchases of these
> grains in order to minimize costs due to spoilage.
> This year, however, fresh oats and corn have
> become the best-selling foods for cattle—a clear
> sign that cattle ranchers are putting nutrition
> ahead of concerns about costs due to spoilage.*

All right. What is the author's conclusion? Go ahead and state it in your own words, then write it here:

You may have written something like, "Cattle ranchers are putting nutrition ahead of cost concerns," or "Cattle ranchers put nutrition ahead of cost." However you stated the conclusion is fine, as long as you understood that the author is trying to convince you that cattle ranchers care more about nutrition than they do about the cost of feed.

Next, since the question tells us to weaken the author's argument, we need to examine the premises the author gave in support of his point. Ask yourself "Why does the author believe cattle ranchers are putting nutrition ahead of cost concerns?" Jot down his premises on a piece of scrap paper.

Hopefully you wrote down something like, "Fresh oats and corn are the most nutritious foods for cattle. Historically, ranchers haven't purchased a lot of them because they spoil. This year fresh oats and corn were the best-selling food for cattle." It is based on the fact that oats and corn are selling so well that the author concludes that cattle ranchers are putting nutrition ahead of cost concerns.

Do you believe the author's argument, based solely on the information he gives you? Are you just going to take his word for it? No, of course not. The author has left some large gaps in the fabric of his argument, and he's relying on you to fill them in with assumptions.

Assumptions are unstated factors in an argument; often they can appear to support the conclusion. The farmer's conclusion, that ranchers are putting nutrition ahead of cost, rests on a single fact; that fresh corn and oats outsold other forms of cattle feed this year, even thought they have historically been more expensive. The author is depending on you to fill in the gap, to supply the missing information that will make his argument work.

What piece of information could you supply to further support the conclusion? Well, you could provide evidence that demonstrates that nutrition is the only reason cattle ranchers are buying fresh corn and oats this year, or you could rule out other reasons for this phenomenon. In any event, we will focus our attack on this weak point; the gap in his argument where the author expects you to do his work for him by filling in assumptions.

Step 3: Answer the Question in Your Own Words

Reread the question (but keep ignoring those answer choices!). It asked us how we might weaken the author's argument. Did anything strike you as incomplete about the argument as you read it? Does the author's reasoning seem sound to you? To weaken an argument, we look for flaws or gaps in the author's reasoning. If we can find another way to reach the same conclusion as the author, or if we can show that the premises the author uses to support his argument are not sound, then we are weakening the argument.

Okay, so we already established that the author expects you to assume that concern about nutrition is the sole reason cattle ranchers are buying more fresh feed. He draws his conclusion, that ranchers are putting nutrition ahead of cost concerns, based on only one piece of evidence: Fresh oats and corn have become the best-selling food for cattle. If the author were sitting right in front of you, what would you say to refute his argument? Can you think of any other reason why corn and oats might be selling better this year? Use this space to jot down any ideas you have on a piece of scrap paper.

You can probably think of a few reasons, such as a higher birthrate among cattle, resulting in more stock to feed, or a lower availability of other foodstuffs. Or you might have said that previous concerns about spoilage had been alleviated, or that the price had dropped to such a degree that ranchers were more willing to risk spoilage. There are a number of possible reasons why fresh corn and oats might have become best-selling foods, besides the author's stated reason. All right—now you're ready to attack those answer choices.

Step 4: Process of Elimination

Since we're going after the weak spots, or assumptions, in the argument, let's look for an answer choice that will drive a wedge between the conclusion and the premises. In fact, as you read each answer choice, you can ask yourself, "Does this weaken it?" If you answer no, eliminate it.

We'll read all five answer choices below. Remember that your job is not to choose the right answer but, by Process of Elimination, to narrow the choices down to the best possible answer. All you know about the fascinating topic of cattle feed is what you've been told by the argument, so make sure you keep your thinking narrow. Let's start.

○ Last year, processed cattle feed outsold fresh oats and corn by a wide margin.

No. We are trying to weaken the argument, so what happened last year does not matter. We want to know what happened this year. Eliminate this answer choice.

○ No cattle ranchers have reported in surveys that they are attempting to purchase more nutritious fodder for their herds.

No. This answer choice actually argues against the conclusion, which is (perhaps surprisingly) never a valid way to weaken an argument. All you do when you argue against the conclusion is set up another line of reasoning that might be just as flawed as the original argument. In this case, for instance, there are all kinds of problems with the validity of surveys, and that alone makes this attack particularly weak. We're better off attacking the issue of whether or not large corn and oat purchases signal that ranchers value nutrition more highly than cost savings.

○ Cattle ranchers are attempting to counter recent claims about the health risks associated with eating beef by becoming more conscious of the nutritive quality of the meat they are producing.

No. This answer choice, in fact, strengthens the position that nutrition is the sole reason cattle ranchers have increased their purchases of fresh fodder. Remember, we're trying to weaken the argument by citing a reason (besides nutrition) why cattle ranchers are buying different feed this year. Eliminate it.

○ Because of crop failures, all types of cattle fodder—including fresh oats and corn, processed cattle feed, and frozen nutritional supplements—were more expensive this year than in previous years.

No. Though this answer choice states that all types of feed are more expensive, it doesn't tell us that the cost of fresh oats and corn were surpassed in cost by the other feeds. It is more likely that oats and corn are still proportionally more expensive than the other feeds. This answer choice doesn't tell us anything about nutrition either, so this doesn't help us weaken the argument. Eliminate it.

○ Because of agricultural innovations, fresh oats and corn spoil much less quickly than in previous years, while the purchase price for such fodder has remained constant.

Okay, that sounds more like it. Now that corn and oats do not spoil as quickly, costs (related to spoilage) are lower. Ranches may or may not value nutrition more highly than monetary savings, but the costs associated with corn and oats have decreased. Cost is no longer a barrier to buying better food, and finally we have a reason, besides nutrition, why cattle ranchers are buying fresh fodder.

So choice (E) is the best answer, if only because there is something wrong with the other four choices.

More on Process of Elimination (POE)

By using the Four-Step approach, you determined that choice (E) was the best answer to the question above. But maybe you're not so sure whether, left on your own, you'd have seen clear reasons for eliminating those four answer choices. So let's take a closer look at some common reasons why we eliminate answer choices in POE.

Scope

You will succeed on arguments only if you are able to keep your focus very narrow. Remember that all you know about the topic in question is what you were told in that paragraph. Put simply, the *scope* of the argument is dictated by the information given in the conclusion and the premises.

With this in mind, let's take another look at answer choice (A). The scope of the cattle feed argument is confined to what has taken place this year, so information about last year is beyond the argument's scope. When you see an answer choice that goes beyond the realm of the argument, you can consider it *out of scope* and eliminate it. Scope is by far the most common reason for eliminating answer choices in the arguments section.

Opposite

When you're dealing with questions that ask you to weaken or strengthen the author's conclusion, be very wary of answer choices that, while within the scope, do exactly the opposite of what you want. Answer choice (C) is a prime example of this. You're looking for a reason, aside from nutrition, to explain why ranchers are buying more fresh feed this year, but answer choice (C) simply gives yet another way in which nutrition is the sole motivational factor. Thus, while it is in the scope of the argument, it is the opposite of the answer choice you want, and you should eliminate it.

Extreme

Extreme wording is another very common reason for eliminating answer choices in POE. Extreme statements, such as "Everybody loves Picasso," can be easily disproved. This, therefore, is not the type of answer choice ETS is likely to count as the credited response.

Go ahead and try the question below. Work through your Four-Step approach on this question, paying special attention to POE when you get to the answer choices.

> *To many environmentalists, the extinction of plants—accompanied by the increasing genetic uniformity of food crops—is the single most serious environmental problem. Something must*

be done to prevent the loss of wild food plants or no-longer-cultivated food plants. Otherwise, the lack of genetic food diversity could allow for significant portions of major crops to be destroyed overnight. In 1970, for example, southern leaf blight destroyed approximately 20 percent of the United States corn crop, leaving very few varieties of corn unaffected, in the areas over which the disease spread.

Which of the following can be inferred from the passage above?

○ Susceptibility to certain plant diseases is genetically determined.

○ Eighty percent of the corn grown in the United States is completely resistant to southern leaf blight.

○ The extinction of wild food plants can be traced back definitively to destructive plant diseases.

○ Plant breeders must focus on developing plants that are resistant to plant disease.

○ Corn is the only food crop threatened by southern leaf blight.

Step 1: Read the Question. This question is an example of a type of question we call "Inference." Much like the Inference questions in reading comprehension portions of the test, these questions ask you not to deduce, but to actually *point to* something in the passage.

Step 2: Break It Down. Since arguments with Inference questions have an extremely narrow scope, read them even more closely than you usually would. As you break down the argument in these types of questions, you may or may not find an actual point. Focus instead on the scope of the argument, the facts presented, and how they fit together.

In the argument above, the scope is a very narrow discussion of the causes of destruction of food crops. Although the first sentence sets the stage for the topic, it does little more than that. The argument presents a concern about a lack of genetic food diversity and its effect on the long-term health of food crops. An example about the southern leaf blight of 1970 is presented to strengthen the argument.

Step 3: Answer the Question in Your Own Words. Because Inference questions hinge on what you know to be true from the facts in the argument, it is hard to anticipate what a good answer choice will look like, or even to state the answer in your own words. But the understanding you gained of the argument's scope and supporting facts will be enough to get you through your POE.

Step 4: Process of Elimination. You will need to read each answer choice very closely, keeping in mind that the only thing you know about corn, food crops, and southern leaf blight is what you've read in the argument. When eliminating answer choices, ask yourself, "Do I know this?" If you cannot actually point to the information from the answer choice somewhere in the argument, you should eliminate it. Also eliminate answer choices that are outside the scope of the argument, or which contain extreme wording. Keeping that in mind, let's look through the answer choices.

○ Susceptibility to certain plant diseases is genetically determined.

Well, maybe. The argument does say, "the lack of genetic diversity could allow a significant portion of a major crop to be destroyed overnight." It isn't great, but we'll keep this answer choice for now.

○ Eighty percent of the corn grown in the United States is completely resistant to southern leaf blight.

No. There are a couple of reasons why this answer choice is no good. First of all, we cannot possibly know that a crop is completely resistant to southern leaf blight. *Completely* is an example of the kind of extreme wording that allows us to eliminate an answer choice. Furthermore, watch out for traps like this one: Just because you know that 20 percent of the U.S. corn crop was destroyed in 1970 doesn't mean that the 80 percent remaining was resistant. Eliminate it.

○ The extinction of wild food plants can be traced back definitively to destructive plant diseases.

No. Again, watch out for extreme wording. Do we know that this is true in all cases, based on the facts in the argument? No, we don't. As we mentioned, extreme wording like this needs only one counterexample to prove it false, so this is the kind of answer choice ETS will not credit. Eliminate it.

○ Plant breeders must focus on developing
plants that are resistant to plant disease.

No. What plant breeders actually do is outside the scope of the
argument—the argument only states that "Something must be done . . ."
Also, watch out for that extreme wording—answer choices that predict
the future or mandate a course of action are too extreme to be the
credited response. Eliminate it.

○ Corn is the only food crop threatened by
southern leaf blight.

No. Isn't it extreme to say that corn was the *only* plant threatened by
southern leaf blight? We know that corn was affected, but we don't
know if the other plants on the planet were, so eliminate it.

This leaves us with choice (A). Admittedly, not the most flashy or
exciting thing about the argument, but definitely something we can
point to as true. This is the way Inference questions typically work—
you'll have to rely heavily on POE, because the "best" answer rarely
jumps out at you; it's most often just an incidental fact or paraphrase.

Taking POE One Step Further

POE works extremely well in helping you narrow down the answer
choices. Often, you'll even be able to eliminate three of the choices right
away using POE, and will be left with two that seem very similar. To
avoid your having to desperately guess, when you're so close to the
credited response, we'll now refine our POE so it can help you discern
between even two answer choices that may seem very similar.

Down to Two Answers

If you tend to find yourself stumped or stalled after having eliminated
three answer choices, try this:

Read over each remaining choice and concentrate on finding the
difference between them. There may be a word, a phrase, or an entire
idea that you missed the first time through. Use this difference to
determine which answer choice to eliminate, and refer back to the
argument if necessary.

Okay, so now try using your Four-Step approach on the following
question:

> Between 1986 and 1991, the restaurant industry
> saw an average table occupancy rate (i.e., percent
> of the time that a table was occupied) of 74
> percent, while the number of meals eaten out by

Americans stayed constant, at an average of 212 meals out per month per 1,000 people. Between 1991 and 1996, however, the average table occupancy rose to 81 percent, while the number of meals eaten by Americans declined to 195 meals out per month per 1,000 people.

Which of the following most contributes to an explanation of the discrepancy between the average table occupancy and the number of meals eaten out in the period from 1991–1996?

○ The average amount of time spent per meal by Americans eating out increased between 1991 and 1996.

○ The proportion of very lengthy meals to somewhat lengthy meals was greater in 1996 than in 1986.

○ The average number of Americans dining out per month tends to decline whenever table occupancy rates increase.

○ The number of meals served between 1986 and 1991 was fewer than the number of meals served between 1991 and 1996.

○ The more tables a restaurant has, the higher its occupancy rate is likely to be.

Step 1: Read the Question. The question asked you to explain a discrepancy in the facts presented by the argument. We call this type of question "Resolve the Paradox." As you read the argument, keep an eye out for facts that are at odd with each other.

Step 2: Break It Down. Paraphrase the discrepancy in the argument. Here's a hint: You will find it on both sides of a conjunction like *however.*

Step 3: Answer the Question in Your Own Words. The scope of a discrepancy or Paradox argument is very narrow—it's usually just the discrepant facts and a detail that might reconcile them. Think about what facts or information would link the disparate facts in the argument. If you know what you're looking for in advance, you'll be more likely to recognize it when you see it.

Step 4: Process of Elimination. Try this on your own. Okay, you probably eliminated (C) because it is too broad and (E) because it is out of scope. Additionally, both answer choices rely on information that's not furnished in the argument. You may also have eliminated (D) because the number of meals served does not affect why the average table occupancy rate went up.

So you're left with choices (A) and (B), which, at first glance, seem very similar. But take a closer look at the two answer choices. They both discuss the length of time per meal, but they differ in that choice (A) talks about the average time per meal, while (B) refers to "very lengthy" versus "somewhat lengthy" meals. Take a closer look at (B) in light of the information presented in the argument. You'll see that nowhere do we find a way to differentiate between "somewhat lengthy" and "very lengthy" meals. We can only say that meals in general must have been longer, which is the information given in answer choice (A).

MORE QUESTION TYPES

The questions on the GMAT fall into predictable patterns; certain *types* of arguments appear again and again on the test. This means that you can learn how to identify and solve them using your Four-Step process. Up to this point, you have already seen three common argument types; Weaken, Inference, and Paradox, and now we'll look at the three that remain:

Strengthen

You've already seen a question in which you were asked to weaken the author's argument, and you did this by attacking a weak spot in the argument, where the test writers expect you to assume something.

The approach to Strengthen questions is similar, but instead of attacking the argument at its weakest point, you'll provide additional information to strengthen the weak point. So, if the author proves his point by making an assumption, you'll include additional data to bolster the assumption. If the author cites a survey in support of his conclusion, you'll give evidence to prove the validity of the survey. If the author draws his conclusion by means of a comparison, you'll cite further similarities to make the analogy stronger.

The most common structure for arguments you'll be asked to strengthen (or weaken) is one in which assumptions are based on a causal link. The underlying assumptions, in a casual argument are that the stated cause is directly responsible for the outcome, and that there is no other cause. Let's take a look at an argument of this type.

A recent article in a prominent medical journal examines rates of colon cancer among both male and female members of the population.

The author, a well-respected cancer researcher, found that, while the majority of colon cancer sufferers are female, the majority of test subjects in clinical trials on colon cancer medication and treatment are male. Specifically, her research revealed that, while the ratio of male test subjects to female test subjects was three to one, women are, in fact, more than twice as likely to be diagnosed with colon cancer than men. The researcher concludes that "Women experience a higher incidence of colon cancer than their male counterparts. This is due to an overreliance in medical research on male test subjects."

The author's conclusion, that women have a higher likelihood of contracting colon cancer than men, is supported mainly by the premise, "while the majority of colon cancer sufferers are female, the majority of test subjects in clinical trials on colon cancer medication and treatment are male." The author states no other cause for the higher incidence of colon cancer among women, and in fact, the conclusion of this argument can only be supported if we assume that the ratio of male to female test subjects alone is enough to cause the higher incidence of colon cancer among females.

An argument like this is weak because its conclusion depends on a causal link. Its assumptions are that (a) the cause is directly responsible for the effect, and (b) nothing else contributes to or is causing the outcome. The cancer researcher's argument can only work if you assume that (a) the higher incidence of cancer in women is caused by the ratio of male to female test subjects, and that (b) nothing else causes this higher incidence of colon cancer among women.

To strengthen an argument like this one, you need to give the assumptions additional support, either by reinforcing the causal link or by discounting alternate causes. A credited response for the argument above might read, "Diagnostic techniques do not differ from men to women, and women are equally as likely to report symptoms that lead to diagnosis as men." In this way, we rule out the possibility that more women seek treatment or that women are more likely to be diagnosed due to a difference in the technology.

Assumption

Another common argument type is one that asks you to identify the underlying assumptions of the argument, or evaluate how each answer choice contributes to the support of the conclusion. In these cases, the best answer is one that states the unspoken assumption in the argument, while staying within the argument's scope. Work through the following argument, using the Four-Step approach.

Serious novelists start writing because of a desire to create a work of art, and therefore they recognize as great literature the works of other novelists who achieve this goal. As a consequence, when a novel becomes a best-seller, the authors of other novels conclude that the best-seller is not truly great literature.

The explanation offered above for the view authors hold of best-sellers assumes that

○   work on a novel that the author hopes will be regarded as great literature must be undertaken in solitude.

○   serious novelists tend not to view as great literature a novel produced by an author whose success they envy.

○   a novelist can produce a best-seller without having already produced great literature.

○   serious novelists believe that those novelists who produce best-sellers must not have aimed at producing a work of art.

○   the claim of a novel to status as great literature cannot be evaluated by individuals who are not themselves serious novelists.

The best answer is choice (D). The question asks us to state an assumption of the argument. The conclusion of the argument is that, when a novel becomes a best seller, other authors do not regard it as great literature. The premise is that serious novelists write because of a desire to create a work of art, and the argument assumes that one cannot simultaneously create a work of art and a best-seller.

Answer choices (A) and (B) are out of the scope of the argument; we are told nothing about solitude or envy. Choice (C) is also out of the scope; we are not talking about the entire works of an author, but one book. Furthermore, we are not looking to support the argument. Answer choice (E) is also out of scope; the argument is concerned with books that become best-sellers, and not those that become great literature. This leaves (D), which is the assumption we were looking for.

Reasoning

The last and least common type of argument is one that deals not with the content of the argument, but with how it is structured. Questions of this type may read:

> Which of the following indicates a flaw in the reasoning above?

> Susan's attempt to counter Tim's claim is best characterized as . . .

> Dan's response has which of the following relationships to Alissa's argument?

> The author makes his point chiefly by . . .

Your Four-Step approach works on arguments of this type as well. The major difference here is that, with a Reasoning question, as you break it down and state the answer in your own words, you will focus more on describing the pattern of reasoning than in paraphrasing the content of the argument. Go ahead and try this one.

TIM: *When a rare tragedy, such as a plane crash, occurs, many people profess a belief that they themselves are more likely to experience such a tragedy and take extraordinary measures to prevent it. This is unfounded, however. Winning a lottery jackpot, an extremely rare event, does not mean you are any more likely to win a second time.*

SUSAN: *I disagree. The belief is well founded. People who sense danger are more likely to trust their instincts and act in such a way as to prevent the danger from befalling them.*

Susan's attempt to counter Tim's argument is best characterized as one that

- ⊜ makes apparent Tim's failure to consider the consequences of such a tragedy to its survivors.
- ⊜ challenges Tim's assumption that the occurrence of a single event is sufficient to predict future occurrences of that event.
- ⊜ questions the appropriateness of the analogy drawn by Tim.
- ⊜ presents an alternate basis for judging the validity of people's reactions.
- ⊜ disputes the meaning of the term "unfounded."

How'd you do? The question asks you to characterize the argument and is, therefore, a Reasoning question—it's more concerned with structure than content. As you break it down, take note of the way Susan fails to address Tim's premise, but instead introduces her own reasoning. In this case, Tim describes behavior in response to a tragedy, and dismisses it as "unfounded" based on his lottery analogy. Susan provides an alternate explanation for people's behavior. As you use Process of Elimination, ask yourself, "Did they do that?" as a way of testing each answer choice. Here we go:

- ⊜ No. Neither of them discusses the effect of tragedy on its survivors. Eliminate it.
- ⊜ No. Susan does not even address Tim's assumption about the frequency or likelihood of the recurrence of such an event in the future. Eliminate it.
- ⊜ No. Susan does not speak about Tim's analogy. Eliminate it.
- ⊜ Yes. Susan presents another explanation for the behavior pointed out by Tim—that people are more likely to trust their instincts and possibly avert misfortune.
- ⊜ No. There is no such dispute in Susan's argument. Eliminate it.

STEP 4

(HOW NOT TO DO) ALGEBRA

The Quantitative section on the GMAT involves an awful lot of what looks like algebra. You can avoid most of the algebra you encounter though, or at least reduce the work you have to do, by ballparking, reasoning through the question, or Plugging In. Plugging In is a revolutionary technique for turning an algebra problem into a plain arithmetic problem. Intrigued? We'll get to Plugging In shortly, but first we have a little business to get out of the way.

SOLVING FOR X

It's unavoidable. You'll have to solve for x, so let's review the drill. You can solve any equation that contains only one variable by *manipulating the equation*. This means that, through a series of basic arithmetic steps, you move all the numerical terms to one side of the equation, isolating the variable on the other side. The most important thing to remember here is that you must treat both sides of the equation the same: If you subtract 3 from one side, you must subtract it from the other.

Let's take a look at the following example:

$$3x + 4 = 10$$

Your goal is to isolate the variable x on one side of the equals sign; start by getting all the numbers together. On the left, you have +4, so subtract 4 from both sides:

$$3x + 4 = 10$$
$$3x = 10 - 4$$
$$3x = 6$$

Hopefully you can look at this and recognize that $x = 2$, but the final step is to divide both sides by 3.

$$\frac{3x}{3} = \frac{6}{3}, \quad x = 2$$

Nicely done. And now, when you encounter plain equations with variables, you'll know exactly what to do. But occasionally you'll see a word problem, which means you'll have to set up your own equation. Let's start by taking a look at problems dealing with percents, which commonly require you to write your own equation.

PERCENTS

Percent means "out of 100." If 82% of the population has Type O blood, then 82 "out of 100" people have Type O blood. A quarter is 25 cents, also known as $\frac{25}{100}$, or 25% of a dollar. Many of the GMAT problems about percents are word problems, and you'll have to start by translating the English into math so that you can solve them. For example:

> Susan spends 40 percent of her salary (after taxes) on rent each month. If she's paid $48,000 per year (after taxes), how much does Susan spend on rent each month?

Susan's salary is $48,000 per year, but she pays her rent by the month. We need to determine what percent of her monthly salary is paid in rent. Susan's monthly salary is $\frac{48,000}{12}$ or $4,000 per month.

To figure out how much of her monthly salary Susan pays in rent, ask yourself: *What is 40 percent of $4,000?* Once you have this, you can turn the question into an equation and solve. Take a look at the translation table below:

English	Translates to
What	x
Is	$=$
Percent	$\left(\dfrac{1}{100}\right)$
Of	$\times$

What is 40 percent of $4,000 becomes $x = 40\left(\dfrac{1}{100}\right) \times 4{,}000.$

Now solve for x:

$$x = \frac{40}{100} \times 4{,}000$$

$$x = \frac{4}{10} \times 4{,}000$$

$$x = \frac{4 \times 4{,}000}{10}$$

$$x = \frac{4 \times 400}{1}$$

$$x = 1{,}600$$

Susan spends $1,600 per month on rent.

Percent Change

Percent change refers to the percentage amount by which something has increased or decreased. Percent change uses the same English-to-math translation as regular percent questions. You just need to make sure you're tracing the increase or decrease of the correct number. For example:

> Sales in a certain retail outlet this year have increased by an average of $500 per day. If this year's sales are averaging $4,500 per day, by what percentage have average daily sales increased over last year?

To translate this problem into math, you need to ask the question, "$500 is what percent of last year's sales?" But you don't know last year's average daily sales; the problem only tells you *this year's* average daily sales. However, given that you know that this year's average daily sales are $4,500, and this number is $500 more than the average daily sales from last year, then you also know that last year's average daily sales were $4,000. Now translate:

$500 is what percentage of $4,000?

$$500 = x\left(\frac{1}{100}\right) \times 4{,}000$$

$$500 = \frac{x}{100} \times 4{,}000$$

$$500 = \frac{4{,}000x}{100}$$

$$500 = 40x$$
$$\frac{500}{40} = x$$
$$x = 12.5$$

So sales are up 12.5%.

PLUGGING IN

You'll see a lot of word problems on the GMAT that look as though you'll need to write out a series of algebraic equations in order to solve them. The good news is you don't have to. You can turn algebra into arithmetic by using the method of Plugging In.

Consider a question such as:

> Martin has s marbles more than Keith does, and p fewer than George. If Martin has m marbles, how many marbles do Keith and George have together?
>
> ○ $m + s + p$
> ○ $m - s + p$
> ○ $3m - s + p$
> ○ $2m - s + p$
> ○ $3m - s - p$

Wouldn't this problem be easier if you just *knew* how many marbles Martin had? Well, since the entire problem is algebraic, the relationship between the number of marbles Martin has and the number of marbles Keith has will always be the same—if Martin has 10 marbles, Keith will have $10 - s$. Let's try just assuming that Martin *does* have 10 marbles, and see what happens.

Give Martin 10 marbles. He has s more than Keith, so let's say $s = 3$ and Martin has 3 more than Keith. Why 3? Why not? So Keith has 7 marbles. Now, p fewer than George? How about 5 fewer than George, so George has 15.

Now let's answer the question. How many marbles do Keith and George have together? Keith has 7 and George has 15, so together they have 22.

But what about those algebraic answer choices? Simple, just plug in the numbers you used in the problem in place of the variables. So plug in 10 for m, 3 for s, and 5 for p. When you find an answer choice that equals 22 marbles, that's it. Check them all to be safe.

(A) $m + s + p$

$\quad 10 + 3 + 5$

That isn't 22. Keep going.

(B) $m - s + p$

$\quad 10 - 3 + 5$

That isn't 22. Keep going.

(C) $3m - s + p$

$\quad 3(10) - 3 + 5$

$\quad 30 + 2$

That isn't 22 either. Keep going.

(D) $2m - s + p$

$\quad 2(10) - 3 + 5$

$\quad 20 + 2$

Yep. That's 22. You have a winner.

(E) $3m + s - p$

$\quad 3(10) + 3 - 5$

And that one isn't 22 either.

So you've turned a nasty algebraic word problem into a simple arithmetic one. Let's recap the steps for Plugging In:

1) Replace all the variables in the problem with numbers.

2) Read through the new problem and answer the question.

3) Plug your numbers into the answer choices and look for your number.

Write everything down. Carefully write everything down on your scratch paper—you need to write down what every variable equals, what every part of the problem equals, and what your answer is. Rewrite every answer choice with your numbers—don't solve in your head.

Plug In friendly numbers. Why Plug In ugly numbers that will only make the arithmetic difficult? For example, if a question asks for the price of something, make it $100, because $100 is easy to work with. In questions about time, Plug In 30 or 60 for the number of seconds or minutes. You get the picture.

Practice makes perfect. Plugging In works even on easy algebraic word problems, and if you don't practice using it on the easy ones, it won't work for you on the hard ones.

How to Spot a Plugging In Problem

Plugging In problems come in many shapes and sizes. The most commonly seen type is a word problem in which you have variables in both the question and the answer choices, as in the problem above, two other types of plugging in problems are the "Hidden" Plugging In problem, and Plugging In on a "Must Be" problem.

Must Be

The following example will show you what we mean.

If x and y are consecutive integers and $x < y$, then $y^2 - x^2$ must be

○ a prime number.

○ an odd number.

○ an even number.

○ the square of an integer.

○ $(y - x)^2$.

The question asks you what *must* be true. You should Plug In on a question like this, but the important difference here is that you'll need to Plug In two times. Here's why:

Let $x = 2$ and $y = 3$ then plug them in to the equation $y^2 - x^2$. This gives you $9 - 4$, which equals 5. But when you go to the answer choices, you'll see that 5 could make the answer either (A) a prime number, or (B) an odd number, so you need to plug in again to eliminate one of those two answer choices. For now, cross out answer choices (C), (D), and (E).

Choose two more numbers, like $x = 4$ and $y = 5$. $y^2 - x^2$ is $25 - 16$, which is 9. Since 9 is an odd number, but it's not prime, you can safely choose (B). When you Plug In the second time, remember to check only the two answer choices you have left!

DATA SUFFICIENCY

Roughly 40 percent of the math problems on the GMAT won't require you to do any problem solving at all. That's good news, right? Data sufficiency is confusing to many mainly because the concept is hard to get used to, and also because data sufficiency requires a very systematic approach.

In data sufficiency questions, the directions are more confusing than the actual problems; in fact, you may notice people around you during the actual GMAT spending as long as ten minutes trying to understand the directions. Aren't you glad you bought this book?

Before we proceed into the more sophisticated types of data sufficiency questions, let's get a handle on those directions. We'll work through a simple example:

What is x?

(1) $2x = 14$

(2) $x + y = 10$

○   Statement (1) ALONE is sufficient, but statement (2) alone is not sufficient to answer the question asked;

○   Statement (2) ALONE is sufficient, but statement (1) alone is not sufficient to answer the question asked;

○   Both statements together are sufficient to answer the question asked, but NEITHER statement ALONE is sufficient;

○   EACH statement ALONE is sufficient to answer the question asked;

○   Statements (1) and (2) together are NOT sufficient to answer the question asked and additional data specific to the problem are needed.

The fundamental question of data sufficiency is, "Does this statement tell me enough that I can answer the question?" And it is absolutely critical that you begin by considering one statement at a time.

Start with statement (1) and cover up statement (2). Statement (1) tells us that $2x = 14$. Does this tell us enough to answer the question "What is x?" Yes it does, so statement (1) is sufficient. This means that, of all the answer choices, only choice (A) "statement (1) alone is sufficient" and choice (D) "statement (1) alone and statement (2) alone are sufficient" are possible answers. Write down all five answer choices on your scratch paper and cross out choices (B), (C), and (E).

Now look at statement (2) and cover up statement (1). Does statement (2), $x + y = 10$, tell us enough to answer the question, "What is x?" No, it does not. So statement (2) alone is *not* sufficient and the answer cannot be (D), it can only be (A).

AD vs. BCE

This is your basic approach to data sufficiency—start with the first statement and determine whether it alone is sufficient. Eliminate the appropriate answers and move on to the second statement. You should memorize the answer choices so that you never have to think about them. If the first statement is sufficient, write down *AD*. Only choice (A) "statement (1) alone" and choice (D) "statement (1) alone and statement (2) alone" are possible answers. If the first statement is not sufficient, then (A) and (D) are *not* possible answers. Write down *BCE*. Therefore, once you determine whether the first statement is sufficient, write down either *AD* or *BCE*, and do your POE from there.

Don't Solve

Now that we've got the directions under control, let's think about data sufficiency questions and what they're actually asking you to do. You'll see data sufficiency questions that ask you about the same topics as the more traditional "problem solving" math questions—averages, probabilities, coordinate geometry, and the like. But there is one important difference: *You do not need to solve data sufficiency questions.* Solving data sufficiency questions wastes time and doesn't help you answer them.

Remember our example above, "What is x?" We don't actually care what x is, because we don't get any credit for knowing what x is; we only get credit for determining whether the data in the statements are sufficient to determine the answer. Many people waste time *solving* data sufficiency questions and ruin their pacing on the Quantitative section.

The other odd thing about data sufficiency questions is that your information comes in two or three parts. The question may give you part of an equation, and each statement may provide you with another part. You have to be resourceful enough to figure out where to get the information you need. Take a look at this example:

If a certain seamstress in a garment shop made 65 coats, what percent of the shop's total output of coats did she make?

1. The shop made a total of 325 coats.
2. The number of coats made by the seamstress represents $\frac{1}{5}$ of the shop's output of coats.

○ Statement (1) ALONE is sufficient, but statement (2) alone is not sufficient to answer the question asked;

○ Statement (2) ALONE is sufficient, but statement (1) alone is not sufficient to answer the question asked;

○ Both statements together are sufficient to answer the question asked, but NEITHER statement ALONE is sufficient;

○ EACH statement ALONE is sufficient to answer the question asked;

○ Statements (1) and (2) together are NOT sufficient to answer the question asked and additional data specific to the problem are needed.

Okay, so based on the question, and using your English-to-math translation table, you'd turn *65 is what percent of the shop's output?* into

$$65 = x\left(\frac{1}{100}\right) \times \textit{the shop's output.}$$ You already have one variable; it's the

one that answers the question *what percentage*, but you're missing the information about the shop's output.

Look at statement (1): It tells you that the shop made 325 coats. Now you have the total and you can proceed with your equation:

$$65 = x\left(\frac{1}{100}\right) \times 325 .$$ That's enough. You know you *can* solve; you don't

have to go ahead and do it.

At this point, you should have written *AD* on your scratch paper. Take statement (2) and start with your original equation:

$$65 = x\left(\frac{1}{100}\right) \times \textit{the shop's output.}$$ Statement (2) tells you that the number

of coats made by the seamstress is $\frac{1}{5}$ of the shop's output. You can figure out the shop's output, and then plug that into the equation

$$65 = x\left(\frac{1}{100}\right) \times \text{the shop's output},$$ or you can stop and reason for a moment. If the seamstress made $\frac{1}{5}$ of all the coats put out by the shop, then you have your answer. $\frac{1}{5} = 20\%$, so statement (2) is sufficient.

Therefore, the answer is D. Don't get so wound up in the layers of data sufficiency questions that you forget to stop and think things out.

What?!?!?!

Some data sufficiency statements are as straightforward as $2x = 14$, while others might as well be written in a foreign language. What if you saw a problem that read:

How many desserts did the caterer serve?

1. The caterer served 3 ice cream dishes and 4 cakes, and nothing else.
2. Es gibt funf struedelen im dem kulschrank.

○ Statement (1) ALONE is sufficient, but statement (2) alone is not sufficient to answer the question asked;

○ Statement (2) ALONE is sufficient, but statement (1) alone is not sufficient to answer the question asked;

○ Both statements together are sufficient to answer the question asked, but NEITHER statement ALONE is sufficient;

○ EACH statement ALONE is sufficient to answer the question asked;

○ Statements (1) and (2) together are NOT sufficient to answer the question asked and additional data specific to the problem are needed.

Well, starting with statement (1) allows you to narrow the answer choices down to *AD*. What if you have absolutely no idea what statement (2) is saying? That's okay. Even though you cannot decipher statement (2), you still have a 50 percent shot, so guess (A) or (D) and go on.

Plugging In on Data Sufficiency

You can (and absolutely should) Plug In on data sufficiency questions, but be careful. You may have to Plug In more than once. Let's look at the following question:

Is $\frac{x}{2}$ an integer?

1. $2x$ is an even integer
2. $2x = 3$

○ Statement (1) ALONE is sufficient, but statement (2) alone is not sufficient to answer the question asked;

○ Statement (2) ALONE is sufficient, but statement (1) alone is not sufficient to answer the question asked;

○ Both statements together are sufficient to answer the question asked, but NEITHER statement ALONE is sufficient;

○ EACH statement ALONE is sufficient to answer the question asked;

○ Statements (1) and (2) together are NOT sufficient to answer the question asked and additional data specific to the problem are needed.

The question is not asking you what $\frac{x}{2}$ is; it's just asking whether $\frac{x}{2}$ is an integer. And whether the answer is yes or no, as long as you can answer definitively one or the other, the data are sufficient.

Start with statement (1), and Plug In. You must Plug In values that make the statement true. For example, you can plug in 2 for x in statement (1), because $2x$ is 4 and that's an even integer. But you cannot plug in $\frac{2}{3}$, because $2\left(\frac{2}{3}\right)$ is not an integer. Now, since 2 is okay for x in statement (1), plug 2 into the question and see what happens.

$$\frac{x}{2} = \frac{2}{2} = 1$$

That's an integer, so the answer is *yes*.

But is the answer *always* yes? Try another number, like 3. We can test statement (1) using 3, because statement (1) stipulates that $2x$ is an integer, and with 3 for x, $2x$ is an integer; it's 6. But when you plug in 3 for x in the question, you get $\frac{x}{2}$, and $\frac{3}{2}$ is not an integer, so the answer is no. This means that statement (1) is not sufficient—plugging in different numbers gives you different answers.

Write down *BCE* and move on to statement (2), which tells you that $2x = 3$. So x can only be $\frac{3}{2}$. No need to plug in here. If x is $\frac{3}{2}$, then you can answer the question *Is $\frac{x}{2}$ an integer?* Statement (2) alone is sufficient and the answer is (B).

STEP 5

FORMULAS

There are certain math concepts that ETS loves to test repeatedly. You probably learned these concepts back in high school, but you may have forgotten them entirely. After all, when was the last time you found the mode of anything? We've simplified each of these concepts down to a formula or a clear-cut, systematic approach that you should memorize or familiarize yourself with. By learning them, you'll be able to deal with averages, rate problems, and even probabilities, no matter how cleverly ETS disguises them.

DISTANCE

Flash back to high school. Remember those dreaded word problems in which train A left the station at 6 P.M. traveling 70 miles per hour, and train B left the station at 5 P.M. traveling 50 miles per hour, and you had to determine at what time train A would overtake train B? Problems like this one, and any problems that involve travel, distance, miles per hour, feet per second, planes, trains, or automobiles on the GMAT can be boiled down to one formula:

$$Distance = rate \times time$$

The problem must give you two of the three variables, so substitute them into the formula and solve. Try this one:

> A plane leaves Chicago at 6 A.M. and is scheduled to arrive in San Francisco, 2,150 miles away, 4 hours later. For the first 2 hours of the trip, the pilot maintains an average speed of 450 miles per

hour. If the flight is to arrive as scheduled, what must the plane's average speed be, in miles per hour, for the next 2 hours?

○ 525
○ 550
○ 600
○ 625
○ 650

As soon as you determine that the problem is about travel, jot down your formula, $d = r \times t$ and fill in what you know. The 4-hour trip is divided into 2 parts, the first 2 hours and the last 2 hours, and the question asks you for the average speed of the last 2 hours.

Start with what you know about the first 2 hours: The rate is 450 mph and the time is 2 hours. Using the distance formula, $d = r \times t$, we get $d = 450 \times 2$, or 900 miles. That's the distance traveled in the first 2 hours.

The distance that remains to be covered in the last 2 hours, then, is 1,250 miles (2,150 – 900). Again, plug what you know in to the distance formula: $d = r \times t$, so $1,250 = r \times 2$. Solve for r, and you'll get the average speed required for the last 2 hours: 625 miles per hour. The answer is (D).

WORK

Work problems are the other type of problems that involve rate on the GMAT. These problems revolve around how quickly a person or machine can complete a job or make a certain number of gadgets, for instance. Although these problems typically involve people or machines working at two different rates for varying lengths of time, it usually all boils down to how much work each can do in one hour. Try this one:

If Anil can finish a job in 4 hours and Gustavo can finish the same job in 6 hours, how long would it take them, working together at their respective rates, to complete the job?

○ 1 hour, 50 minutes
○ 2 hours, 10 minutes
○ 2 hours, 30 minutes
○ 3 hours, 45 minutes
○ 4 hours, 30 minutes

If Anil can complete the entire job in 4 hours, then he does $\frac{1}{4}$ of the job per hour. Gustavo, then, does $\frac{1}{6}$ of the job per hour. So working together, how much of the job can they do in one hour? First add up their rates, using the Bowtie: $\frac{1}{4} + \frac{1}{6} = \frac{6+4}{4 \times 6} = \frac{10}{24} = \frac{5}{12}$.

This means that, in 1 hour, Anil and Gustavo together can do $\frac{5}{12}$ of the job. In two hours, then, they can do $\frac{10}{12}$ of the job, leaving $\frac{2}{12}$ of the job to do. What is $\frac{2}{12}$, or $\frac{1}{6}$ of an hour? It's 10 minutes. So Anil and Gustavo, working together at their respective rates, can complete the job in 2 hours, 10 minutes, and the answer is (B).

GROUPS

Remember these?

> In a group of 60 children, $\frac{7}{12}$ are girls, $\frac{2}{3}$ are right-handed and $\frac{2}{5}$ are right handed-girls. How many of the children are left-handed boys?
>
> ○ 36
> ○ 24
> ○ 19
> ○ 16
> ○ 9

To tackle a problem like this one, use the formula:

$$Group_1 + Group_2 + Neither - Both = Total$$

Group 1 is made up of the children who are girls ($\frac{7}{12}$ of 60, or 35 children) and group 2 is made up of the children who are right-handed ($\frac{2}{3}$ of 60, or 40 children). You know the number of children who are both girls and right-handed ($\frac{2}{5}$ of 60, or 24 children). You also know the total number of children is 60. Great—you have everything you need to answer the question.

The question asks how many of the children are left-handed boys, so it's really asking how many of the children are neither right-handed not girls. That's the *Neither*, and that's what you'll solve for. Go ahead and fill in the formula with what you know.

$$Group_1 + Group_2 + Neither - Both = Total$$

$$35 + 40 + Neither - 24 = 60$$

$$75 - 24 + Neither = 60$$

$$51 + Neither = 60$$

$$Neither = 9$$

Nine children are neither right-handed nor girls (they're left-handed boys), and our answer is choice (E).

AVERAGE

The *average*, or arithmetic mean, of a set of numbers is the sum of the numbers divided by the number of them in the set. This can be represented by the formula $A = \frac{T}{N}$, where A = Average, T = Total (the sum of all the numbers), and N = the number of numbers you're averaging.

Try this question:

> In a certain month, a pizzeria sold 75 pizzas in the first week, twice as many in the second week as in the first, two-thirds more in the third week than in the first, and three-fifths as many in the fourth week as in the second. What is the average number, per week, of pizzas sold by the pizzeria?
>
> ○   100
> ○   105
> ○   110
> ○   115
> ○   120

This problem looks tougher than it is. Start by writing down the formula and then fill in what you know:

$$A = \frac{T}{N}$$

You know N (the number of weeks) is 4, and the question asks you for A, the average. Based on the information given, then, you must be able to determine the total number of pizzas sold. The total is the sum of the number of pizzas sold in each of the 4 weeks. To figure that out, read slowly through the information given, and take careful notes to avoid mistakes.

Week 1 = 75

Week 2 = twice Week 1, or 150

Week 3 = $\frac{2}{3}$ more than Week 1, so $75 + \frac{2}{3}(75) = 75 + 50 = 125$

Week 4 = $\frac{3}{5}$ of Week 2, or $\frac{3}{5}(150) = 90$

You now know the total number of pizzas sold: $75 + 150 + 125 + 90$, or 440. Plug this number into the formula, and solve for the average, A.

$$A = \frac{T}{N}$$
$$A = \frac{440}{4}$$
$$A = 110$$

The answer is choice (C).

On the GMAT, you may also see the terms *mode, median,* and *range* in questions about sets of numbers. The *mode* is the number or term in a set that occurs most frequently. The *median* is the number in the middle of the set, after you've arranged the numbers in ascending order. The *range* is the difference between the high and low values of a set.

So, for the following set of numbers, can you determine the mode, median, and range?

{25, 13, 36, 25, 40, 25, 13}

Mode: 25 is the mode, because it is the number that appears most frequently in this set.

Median: First arrange the numbers in ascending order:

{13, 13, 25, 25, 25, 36, 40}

The fourth number of this seven-number set, 25, is the median. Had there been an even number of terms in the set, the median would have been the average of the two middle numbers.

Range: The highest number in the set is 40, and the lowest is 13, so the range is their difference, 27.

RATIO

A *ratio* is just another way of representing sizes of parts of a whole. A ratio is always expressed as the relationship of parts to parts (not parts to whole, like a fraction), in lowest terms. Say that, in a bowl of 40 jellybeans, 16 are red and the rest are green. The ratio of red to green jellybeans, then, is 2:3 (16 red jellybeans and 24 green jellybeans, or 16:24, which can be reduced to 2:3).

You can add all the parts in a ratio to determine the total number of items in the ratio. For example, if a fruit salad contains raisins, grapes, pineapple chunks, and apricots in a ratio of 2:6:5:3, the total number of pieces of fruit in the salad is the sum of the parts, or $2 + 6 + 5 + 3 = 16$.

PROBABILITY

Probability is simply the likelihood that a certain event will occur. Think about rolling a conventional six-sided die, for example. The probability of rolling a 4 is 1 in 6, because there are 6 possible faces, and only 1 of them is a 4. Probability is expressed as a fraction in lowest terms, so the probability of rolling a 4 on a six-sided die is $\frac{1}{6}$.

Try this example:

> In a certain raffle, 500 tickets are sold. Bob purchases 280 of the tickets. What is the probability that one of Bob's tickets will be drawn?

Take the number of possible outcomes that work, 280, put it in a fraction over 500, and reduce: $\frac{280}{500} = \frac{28}{50} = \frac{14}{25}$

So, as you can see, Bob has a 14-in-25 chance of winning the lottery. That makes sense—Bob has more than half the tickets, so he has more than a 50-percent shot at winning.

On the GMAT, you might have to figure out the probability of a series of things happening. Remember our six-sided die? The probability of throwing a 4 was $\frac{1}{6}$, but say you have to determine the probability of throwing a 4 on three successive throws. Just multiply the probabilities of each individual throw: $\frac{1}{6} \times \frac{1}{6} \times \frac{1}{6} = \frac{1}{216}$. So there is a 1-in-216 chance of throwing a 4 three times in a row.

You may also be asked to determine probability as the number of things changes. For example:

> There are a total of 10 sandwiches in a picnic hamper, 5 of which are ham, 3 of which are roast beef, and 2 of which are turkey. If 3 of the sandwiches are removed at random, what is the probability that all 3 roast beef sandwiches are removed?
>
> ○ $\frac{3}{10}$
>
> ○ $\frac{2}{45}$
>
> ○ $\frac{3}{80}$
>
> ○ $\frac{1}{27}$
>
> ○ $\frac{1}{120}$

Start by determining the probability that the first sandwich is roast beef; it's $\frac{3}{10}$. Now start over with what you have left: 9 sandwiches, 2 of which are roast beef. This makes the probability of getting roast beef the second time $\frac{2}{9}$. Now you have 8 sandwiches left, and only 1 is roast beef, so the probability of choosing it is $\frac{1}{8}$. To determine the probability of getting roast beef all three times, multiply the individual probabilities together and reduce: $\frac{3}{10} \times \frac{2}{9} \times \frac{1}{8} = \frac{1}{120}$, so the answer is (E).

FOIL

FOIL stands for First, Outer, Inner, Last, and is the process by which you can multiply two terms that look like this: $(a - 3)(a + 5)$. FOIL reminds you to multiply the first parts of the terms together, then the outer parts, then the inner parts, and finally the last parts of the two terms. It goes like this:

$$(a - 3)(a + 5)$$

First: $a \times a = a^2$

Outer: $a \times 5 = 5a$

Inner: $-3 \times a = -3a$

Last: $-3 \times 5 = -15$

Combine the terms and simplify:

$$a^2 + 5a - 3a - 15 = a^2 + 2a - 15$$

FACTORING

Factoring is pretty much just FOIL in reverse. Start by setting up the parentheses and then work backward to figure out the values of the two expressions that must have been multiplied together:

$$x^2 - x + 12 = 0$$

What two first terms have been multiplied to get x^2? Yes, x and x. Put them in your parentheses as your first terms:

$$(x \quad)(x \quad)$$

Now try to determine which signs go in the middle, based on the sign of the middle and last terms. Your last term, 12, is positive, but your middle term, $-7x$, is negative, so two negative numbers must have been multiplied together in order to get your last term. Put the negative signs in your parentheses.

$$(x - \quad)(x - \quad)$$

Now, to find the last terms, you have to determine what could have been multiplied together to give you 12, but you must keep the Outer/Inner combinations in mind. 12 is the product of $1 \times 12, 2 \times 6$, and 3×4. Which set of factors, when added, give you $7x$? That's right; 3 and 4. Place them in the parentheses and you're done:

$$(x - 3)(x - 4)$$

STEP 6

READING
COMPREHENSION

You know how to read, right? You've been doing it for years. Then what makes the reading comprehension questions on the GMAT so tough?

Well, for starters, the clock is ticking. The passages are dense and, in many cases, boring. You may find that the questions are difficult to understand, and the answer choices all seem to say the same thing. You may be relieved to learn that in order to be successful on reading comprehension questions, you'll just need to hone your skills in skimming and eliminating, not practice endurance. Sound promising?

Reading comprehension passages on the GMAT are 200 to 350 words long, and you'll see as many as four of them, each of which will be followed by three or four questions. Business, science, and social science are the most commonly discussed topics, but no specialized knowledge of any of these fields is necessary.

Take a look at a typical GMAT reading comprehension passage. We'll refer back to it in the pages to come.

> The Japanese system of *kanban* (just-in-time inventory control), credited for much of the Japanese automobile industry's success in the 1980s, may be falling out of favor. The large-scale demands of international trade reward more planned schedules of production and have led to a reintroduction of an old friend: the specialized worker.

The conflict between most marketing and production departments is well documented. Marketing departments need to respond quickly to changing customer wants and needs; production departments need to plan their production on a two-week schedule, with each department informing other departments of its backlogs, inventories, and outputs. To make the *kanban* system work, however, the manufacturers had to train production employees to shift on a moment's notice to any job in the factory, as needed, thus diminishing the role of the specialized worker.

But *kanban* may have caused its own demise. By being so efficient and responsive, Japanese automobile manufacturers find themselves confronted with a large and predictable global demand. Requests for automobiles are increasing at such a steady rate that managers can now determine production schedules up to ten months in advance and, as a result, workers no longer need to jump from position to position. Since long-term scheduling has become possible, productivity has risen 27 percent.

If you're like most people, you read through that passage slowly and painstakingly, trying to assimilate all the information and commit the details to memory. If you do this, chances are you won't remember much, and the questions won't ask you about the stuff you do remember. To top it off, you'll have wasted three to five minutes on the passage, which will make you pressed for time and more likely to rush through the questions, missing most of them.

YOUR MISSION

You don't get points on the GMAT for reading the passage; you get points for answering the questions correctly. The Four-Step approach we're going to teach you focuses on the questions, not the passage. In fact, we don't even want you to read the passage!

THE FOUR-STEP APPROACH

Don't think of this as "reading comprehension," think of it as an open book test. The answers to each question are somewhere in the passage—your job is to find them as quickly as you can.

Step 1: Read and Understand the Question

This is very important: Read the question first. Don't just skim the question; really make sure you grasp what it's asking you. Most of the time you'll just need to <u>locate a specific piece of information in the passage and use it to answer the question</u>. Ignore the answer choices for now—they'll distract you. Cover them up with your hand if necessary.

Step 2: Find the Answer in the Passage

Now you can read the passage with the question in mind, or even skim it if you're comfortable doing that. Look for the term or idea around which the question centers. When you've found the correct part of the passage read it carefully. Don't just read the sentence the term is located in—read the ones immediately before and after it for maximum comprehension.

Step 3: State the Answer in Your Own Words

Now reread the question (not the answer choices) and answer it in your own words, based on what you just read. Write down your answer so you can refer back to it.

Step 4: Process of Elimination (POE)

Finally you can look at the answer choices. Read each one carefully; if it is similar to what you jotted down, keep it. If not, eliminate it. (You can also use POE to eliminate answer choices, for more obvious reasons—more on this later.)

If none of the answer choices matches, the idea that the question centers on might also be discussed in another place in the passage. Return to the passage and look for such a place. You also might have misread something; remember, it is okay to refer to the passage. Our goal is to minimize rereading, not eliminate it altogether.

READING COMPREHENSION QUESTION TYPES

Specific Questions

Now that you're well acquainted with the Four-Step approach, let's try it out on some questions. The majority of the questions on the GMAT will be *Specific*, which means that they'll ask you about a Specific term or idea in the passage, rather than the passage as a whole.

Specific questions center on a key word or idea. For example, if the question reads, "The author most likely mentions Hammurabi's Code in order to . . ." your key phrase is *Hammurabi's Code*. Write that down on your scratch paper, and skim the passage looking for *Hammurabi's Code*. When you're ready to use POE, you can eliminate answer choices that do not pertain to Hammurabi's Code, as well as ones that refer to parts of the passage in which Hammurabi's Code is not discussed.

Try out the Four-Step approach on this question, which is based on the sample passage about the Japanese automotive industry:

> It can be inferred from the passage that the conflict between marketing departments and production departments
>
> ○ resulted from both departments' failure to communicate concerning backlogs, inventories, and outputs.
>
> ○ led to the training of marketing employees in the *kanban* system, enabling them to shift rapidly to any job in the factory.
>
> ○ stemmed from the production departments' need to schedule and the marketing departments' need to respond quickly.
>
> ○ rested on the shortened two-week timeframe of the *kanban* system.
>
> ○ was the primary reason for the lack of success of the Japanese automobile industry in the 1980s.

Step 1: Read and Understand the Question. *Marketing departments and production departments* is your key phrase; the question asks you what caused the conflict between them. Write something to this effect on your scratch paper.

Step 2: Skim the Passage. You will find your key words in the second sentence of the second paragraph. Read the sentences before and after this sentence (so the first and third).

Step 3: Answer the Question in Your Own Words. Reread the question and answer it in your own words. For example, you may have written, *the departments had different needs*. One of the answer choices should match that pretty closely.

Step 4: Process of Elimination. Now let's look at each answer choice individually and eliminate those that don't sound close to what you've written down as your answer. Go ahead and write *ABCDE* on your scratch paper.

(A) No. The passage never stated that the two departments failed to communicate. Eliminate it.

(B) No. This is a misrepresentation of information in the passage. The employees were trained for manufacturing, not marketing. Eliminate it.

(C) Yes. This is directly stated in the part of the passage that you read.

(D) No. *Kanban* solved the problem; it didn't create it. Eliminate it.

(E) No, just the opposite. It was a primary factor in the success of the industry in the 1980s. Eliminate it.

So (C) is the best answer.

Let's try another question, again based on the *kanban* passage:

> The author cites the productivity increase of 27 percent in order to
>
> ○ prove the argument that *kanban* workers are more efficient than specialized workers.
>
> ○ provide an example of how rapid response to global demands can improve productivity.
>
> ○ argue against the reintroduction of the specialized worker.
>
> ○ support the thesis that predictable demand may encourage an otherwise less efficient practice.
>
> ○ challenge the theory that *kanban* workers are less efficient in a global market.

This question asks about what the author does, so you need to be conscious of just how short a GMAT passage is. The author only has about 250 words—he can illustrate, illuminate, and elucidate; display, discuss, or divulge. The author cannot prove, refute, resolve, or define—not in 250 words. So keep that in mind as you work through your Four-Step process, and especially as you use POE.

Here we go:

(A)   No. The word *prove* makes this answer choice too extreme. Furthermore, this was never stated in the passage. Eliminate it.

(B)   No. Rapid response is no longer needed because scheduling is long term. Eliminate it.

(C)   No. According to the passage, there is no reason to argue against the reintroduction of the specialized worker. Eliminate it.

(D)   Yes. This shows that specialized workers, an otherwise less efficient organizational choice, can function well under long-term scheduling. Keep it.

(E)   No. No such theory is ever posited. Eliminate it.

The best answer is choice (D).

Getting the hang of it? Great, let's try one more:

> It can be inferred from the passage that specialized workers
>
> ○   require more training than employees under the *kanban* system.
>
> ○   play a more limited role in the *kanban* system.
>
> ○   are only useful when long-term planning becomes possible.
>
> ○   respond to changes in demand quickly and efficiently.
>
> ○   handle backlog and inventory problems more efficiently than do *kanban*-trained workers.

A question like the one above can be tricky. If you had insisted on reading and committing to memory every word in the passage, then every answer choice would have sounded good. But thankfully, you remembered to use the key phrase, *specialized workers,* and so you'll concentrate only on the part of the passage containing that phrase.

(A)   No. Training is never mentioned in the passage. Eliminate it.

(B)   Yes. The passage states this in lines 16-21. Keep it.

(C)   No. The word *only* makes this answer choice extreme. Eliminate it.

(D)   No. Marketing departments must respond to changes quickly.

Eliminate it.

(E)   No. Handling backlog problems efficiently is not discussed anywhere in the passage. Eliminate it.

Answer choice (B) is the best answer.

General Questions

A General question is one that asks you about the main idea, theme, or tone of the entire passage. Since this type of question asks you to consider the entire passage, the best answer will also encompass the entire passage. Answer choices that refer only to one part of the passage are too specific to be correct, so you can eliminate them. Also, get rid of answer choices that are too vast or general for the author to accomplish in 250 words. Consider the following answer choice: "The author traces the evolution of the relationship between the New York Stock Exchange and the Federal Reserve System, and resolves the interdependent role of interest rates in both." This just can't be done in 250 words.

Answers to General questions will be (not surprisingly) less definitive than those to specific questions. The best answer will be true but noncommittal. Answer choices that contain words such as *always, never, must, every,* and *complete* are too definitive, so eliminate them—if an answer choice can be refuted so easily, ETS will not credit it.

As we said, a General question is one that asks you about the main idea, theme, or tone of the entire passage. While there is obviously no single place in the passage that contains the answer to a General question, you can still answer these questions using the Four-Step approach. We'll show you how, but first, a few more points about General questions.

Even though they ask about the entire passage, General questions will not require you to *read* the whole passage. If you've already answered a couple of specific questions about the passage, you may already have a very good idea of what it's about, so review the answers you jotted down and use POE. Or go back to the passage and read the first sentence of each paragraph and the last sentence of the entire passage—this will give you a better sense of the passage as a whole.

Using what you now know about general questions, let's look at the *kanban* passage and try a General question:

The passage is primarily concerned with

○ pointing out the variety of management styles at work in the automobile industry.

○ establishing *kanban* as a viable option in the automobile industry.

○ illustrating the effects of *kanban* on employee training.

○ showing that *kanban* can work only in the Japanese automobile industry.

○ describing how a business practice can render itself obsolete.

The phrase *primarily concerned* is very similar to *the main idea, author's purpose,* or *main theme.* Reviewing the answers you jotted down for the previous three questions should be enough to give you a sense of the passage's main idea.

(A) No. This answer choice is too broad. The passage is about *kanban,* not the automobile industry as a whole. Eliminate it.

(B) No. The passage cannot "establish *kanban* as a viable option," because *kanban* has been in use for over a decade. Furthermore, it is unlikely that a 250-word GMAT reading comprehension passage will be the definitive authority on anything. Eliminate it.

(C) No. This is too specific. The passage mentions employee training (among other things), but employee training is not the primary topic of the passage. Eliminate it.

(D) No. The word *only* makes this answer choice too extreme. Remember, ETS will not credit an answer choice that's so easy to disprove. Eliminate it.

(E) Yes. This is the main purpose of the passage, and it is summed up nicely in the first paragraph. This is the best answer.

STEP 7

ANALYTIC WRITING
ASSESSMENT

ISN'T THE GMAT MULTIPLE CHOICE?

The first scored section of the computerized GMAT is called the Analytical Writing Assessment, or AWA. The AWA is made up of two 30-minute essays and is ETS's way of introducing a nonobjective measure into their multiple-choice test. On what barely passes for a word processor, you'll type your answers to two questions in essay form.

The first of these questions, called Analysis of an Issue, asks you to choose one side of a situation and argue it. You will determine whether you agree or disagree with the statement and structure your essay in such a way as to defend the side you've chosen.

The other essay, Analysis of an Argument, asks you to support or attack an argument's line of reasoning. Your job is to critique the author's reasoning—how he structured and supported his argument.

How's It Scored?

Each of your essays will be graded on a scale of 0 (incomprehensible) to 6 (clearly argued and thoughtfully composed). A human reader, who spends about 90 seconds reading each of your essays, and a computer, which spends considerably less time, assign your scores. Unless there is a discrepancy of more than one point (in which case a second human reader assigns a third score), the scores for the two essays are averaged to generate your overall AWA score. Your AWA score is reported separately and is not in any way factored into your scaled overall score (200 to 800).

WHY HAVE THE AWA?

Many theories exist to account for the addition of the AWA essays to the GMAT in 1996. Some argue that the writing assessment was added at the request of business schools, who realized that they'd launched generation after generation of CEOs who couldn't write a proper sentence. A more feasible explanation, however, is that since the 1980s b-schools have been inundated with applicants from abroad, all with varying degrees of fluency in English. Business schools wanted a sure-fire method of determining the fluency of their applicants, and a measure against which to compare the essays in the application (to ensure that the applicants authored their own application essays).

Whatever the reason for their existence, it is important to remember the role these essays play in your admission to business school. Schools don't even see the transcript of your essays unless they request it. Most b-schools simply compare the score against the essays in your actual application. If your application essays are scripted in prose that sings off the page, but your AWA score is a 1 or 2, a b-school might consider asking for another writing sample just to verify that you wrote the essays in your application. If English is not your first language, expect b-schools to look more closely at your AWA essays. As long as your essays are at the same level of writing as your application essays, you have nothing to worry about. B-schools know you're writing the AWA under pressure, and that you're nervous about the multiple-choice portion of the test that's still to come; don't worry, they'll take all that into account.

A handful of business schools will give you the option of substituting your AWA essays for one of the required essays in your application, but it would be foolish to do so. The essays in your application are your opportunity to showcase your talents and experience, while the essays of the AWA are simply an exercise in which you agree or disagree with a specious argument made by some unknown writer at ETS.

THE ENVIRONMENT

Once you've progressed through the tutorial (the untimed portion of the test, in which you're instructed in how to use a mouse, how to scroll, etc.), you'll face the AWA. You'll have 30 minutes to type in your answer for each of the two questions.

On this portion of the test your word-processing functions are limited to these normal keyboard functions:

Enter:	moves the cursor to the beginning of the next line
Backspace:	removes the character to the left of the cursor
Delete:	removes the character to the right of the cursor
Arrows:	moves the cursor up, down, to the left, or to the right
Page Up:	moves the cursor up one page
Page Down:	moves the cursor down one page
End:	moves the cursor to the end of the line of type
Home:	moves the cursor to the beginning of a line of type

In addition to the keyboard commands above, you'll also see three icons on your screen:

Cut:	Drag your mouse (holding down the mouse button) across all the text you want to move. Then click on the *cut* icon. The text you selected will disappear, but it will be stored in the computer's memory.
Paste:	Use the mouse to move your cursor to the place you'd like to insert the text you've cut, and click the *paste* icon. This will cause the text you cut to be inserted at that spot.
Undo:	If you cut or pasted text inadvertently, use the *undo* icon to reverse your most recent action. You can also use *undo* to remove words you've just typed.

These commands may work differently from what you're accustomed to. Keep that in mind as you start to type your essays; do not become flustered or frustrated if you make a mistake.

OVERALL STRATEGY

We'll get into specific strategies for each type of essay in the next few pages, but before you get started, here are some general pointers:

1. **Polish your typing skills.** If you are not in the habit of using a keyboard on a regular basis, take every opportunity between now and test day to practice. We're not suggesting you sign up for a typing class tomorrow, but anything you can do to make the test easier for yourself is a good idea. Although you can probably finish your essays in the allotted time using the old "two finger" method, the more comfortable you are typing, the less stressed you'll be.

2. **Know where you are.** The two AWA essays are very different. The approach you'll use for Analysis of an Issue will be very different from the approach you'll use for Analysis of an Argument. Make sure you know which question you're answering before you proceed.

3. **Choose a side, definitively.** You will actually lose points by arguing both sides of your Issue, or by seeing both strengths and weaknesses in your Argument. It doesn't matter which side you choose, but it does matter that you choose one before you start writing.

4. **Plan your attack.** Start each essay by jotting down four or five points in support of the side of the Issue or Argument you've chosen to defend. Plan to spend at least five minutes on this part of the process. If you brainstorm first, you'll write a better-supported, more organized essay than you will if you jump in and start writing immediately.

5. **Organize your thoughts.** Take the three best points from your brainstorming and transform them into an outline. Decide which point most strongly supports your side and put it first.

6. **Use standard essay format.** Using an introduction, one supporting point per paragraph, and a conclusion, for an overall essay of five to six paragraphs, will help you stay focused as you write, and your essay will be cohesive, organized, and easy to follow. We also recommend you "signpost" along the way, using phrases like *thus* and *primarily* to let your readers know exactly where they are and what to expect next. We'll explore this idea further a little later.

7. **Introduce and conclude first.** Although 30 minutes may seem like plenty of time, your reader will be disappointed if you write a well-supported, intelligent essay, but run out of time before you get to the conclusion. An essay without a conclusion will receive a lower score. You can avoid this by writing the introduction and conclusion first, and using the *cut* and *paste* functions to insert the supporting paragraphs. This may also help you stay organized.

8. **Keep it simple.** Your readers spend about 90 seconds per essay evaluating your writing ability. Complicated sentence construction or 25-cent words, especially if you misuse them, will slow down and distract your readers, and may wear on their patience. You will almost surely be graded down for long-windedness, meandering sentence structure, or wordiness.

9. **Watch your language.** ETS graders are instructed to ignore minor errors in spelling and grammar. Still, unless you are absolutely sure of the spelling of a word, do not use it. If this means your essay is written exclusively in a one- and two-syllable vocabulary, so be it. You are better off coherently arguing your point with small words used and spelled correctly than with fancy ones that are used incorrectly and spelled wrong.

10. **Proofread.** Watch the clock, and leave yourself a few minutes at the end of your half-hour to proofread. No matter how careful a typist you are, you will make mistakes. Give yourself time to catch and correct them so you can present yourself in the best light. If you have trouble proofreading your own writing, and many people do, try reading one word at a time, backwards.

AWA ARGUMENT

The Analysis of an Argument essay asks you to critique someone else's point of view. You are not asked to give your opinion on the topic of the argument; rather, your job is to evaluate how well the author supported his or her opinion.

In this portion of the AWA, you will be presented with an argument very similar to the ones you'll see in the verbal section of the test. Each argument will have a conclusion and premises that the author has chosen to support his or her conclusion. You'll need to take apart this argument to determine how well it is reasoned. But remember, whether or not you agree with the author's conclusion is irrelevant.

The strategy you'll use to analyze the author's argument is very similar to the technique you learned to break down an argument in the critical reasoning section. You'll need to:

Identify the conclusion of the argument, as well as the premises used to support that conclusion.

Point out the assumptions that are necessary for the argument's conclusion to be logically drawn.

Decide how valid the premises and assumptions are, and how well they support the argument.

Identify any places where you find the author's reasoning to be weak and discuss how you would make it stronger.

Keep your opinion to yourself. The biggest mistake test-takers make is to get involved in the argument. Your job is to critique the author's reasoning, not to make his argument for him.

Let's start with a sample question, and proceed through the building of an Analysis of the Argument essay.

The state of Vermont, citing the high injury and fatality rate in motorcycle accidents, recently proposed a law requiring helmets for all motorcycle drivers. Although helmets are typically instrumental in preventing the type of fatalities associated with motorcycle accidents, the law poses an unnecessary restriction and should not be passed. The state of Vermont already requires all motorcycle operators to be over the age of 18, an age where they are considered adults, responsible for making decisions about their own welfare. Furthermore, the majority of motorcycle accidents result in fatality only to the operators of the motorcycle, and many of those fatal accidents do not even involve another vehicle, as they occur when the motorcycle collides with a stationary object.

Discuss how well reasoned you find this argument. In your discussion be sure to analyze the line of reasoning and the use of evidence in the argument. For example, you may need to consider what questionable assumptions underlie the thinking and what alternative explanations or counterexamples might weaken the conclusion. You can also discuss what sort of evidence would strengthen or refute the argument, what changes in the argument would make it more logically sound, and what, if anything, would help you better evaluate its conclusion.

All of the arguments in the AWA section are presented in a standard format. Your response, therefore, should follow a standard essay format. This will make it easier for you to practice writing a good essay, and also make your essay easier to follow.

Let's start by taking this argument apart. First isolate the author's conclusion and jot it down here. Remember, if you have trouble separating the conclusion from the premises, use the "Why" test.

Conclusion:

Did you say that the author believes the law requiring a helmet for anyone operating a motorcycle should not be passed? Good. Now write down, in your own words, the premises the author uses to support his conclusion. Remember to keep your personal opinions on helmet laws to yourself.

Premise 1:

Premise 2:

Premise 3:

Premise 4:

First of all, the author cited the fact that most motorcycle accidents result in the death of only the motorcycle's driver. Furthermore, the author claims that most of the accidents occur when the motorcycle collides with a stationary object. Another of the author's premises is that Vermont already requires motorcycle operators to be over 18, and that 18-year olds are considered adults, responsible for their own welfare. And finally, he states that this made the law redundant and unnecessary.

As you were writing down those premises, you probably noticed that the author relied heavily upon certain assumptions, and you may have even thought of some flaws in the logic of the argument. What were they?

Assumptions or Flaws:

The author bases his argument on some rather weak reasoning. He makes several assumptions, among them are:

- The only reason for passing the helmet law is to prevent fatalities of motorcycle drivers.

- There is no other reason for passing the helmet law, such as cutting down expenses to taxpayers.

- Someone who is considered an adult will make responsible decisions about his or her own welfare and the welfare of others.

- Fatalities are the only degree of injury associated with motor- cycle accidents.

If you got even half of those, you're in good shape. Let's forge ahead into the writing of the actual essay.

The Format

Keep in mind that the *human* essay readers have a very short attention span, and that they read as many as 40 AWA essays an hour. They appreciate a formulaic approach, because it makes it easier for them to assess your essay using standard criteria, and to compare it to the other essays they have seen. Your *computer* reader, or e-rater, is even more dogmatic. It has read hundreds of human-scored sample essays on the topic you're writing about, and has developed a series of criteria that good essays all meet.

We said you should write your essay using a standard format, including an introduction, three supporting paragraphs, and a conclusion. Now let's look more closely at what role these three components should perform.

Introduction

Your introduction should quickly recap the author's point and indicate the direction your essay will take. Remember that your job is to identify weaknesses in the author's logical construction. Write your introduction on a piece of scrap paper, then continue.

A good introductory paragraph for our motorcycle argument might read:

> The author states that the state of Vermont's proposed helmet law is redundant and unnecessary and should not be passed. This conclusion is based on faulty reasoning and invalid assumptions, which do not lend sufficient support to the author's thesis.

Body Paragraphs

Choose the three strongest or clearest points from your brainstorming—the points you think weaken the author's argument most effectively. You'll explore these points in your three body paragraphs, each of which should address a different point using two to three sentences. You can evaluate the believability of the author's assumptions, make suggestions for improving the argument by filling in gaps left by assumptions or correcting faulty reasoning. Make sure to use details and examples to strengthen your essay. Also, show your reader where you're going by using words like *first*, *additionally*, *furthermore*, and *however*. Try a couple of body paragraphs now, and then take a look at what we've done.

Okay, we think a good body paragraph starts like this:

"One of the largest flaws in the argument is that it relies upon the assumption that . . . ."

or

"Furthermore, the author assumes that [assumption]. He fails to consider the possibility, however, that . . . ."

Conclusion

The concluding paragraph is your opportunity to really drive your point home. It is the last impression your reader will have of your writing, so make it strong. You should begin with clear conclusion words, such as *in conclusion, clearly,* or *therefore*. Sum up the criticism you made of the argument and make final recommendations for improvement.

Craft a brief conclusion, and then take a look at what we did. Here's ours:

The author's argument against the state of Vermont's proposed helmet law, therefore, is flawed and implausible, as it relies on a series of unsubstantiated premises and fallacious reasoning.

Putting It All Together

As you look over our sample Analysis of an Argument essay to see how closely yours compares, keep in mind that it's more important that your structure and signposting are similar to ours than that you chose the same assumptions or weak spots in reasoning to attack.

Our Sample Analysis of an Argument

The author says that the state of Vermont's proposed helmet law is redundant and unnecessary and should not be passed. This conclusion is based upon faulty reasoning and invalid assumptions, which do not lend sufficient support to the author's thesis. The author bases his conclusion on facts about the fatality rate in motorcycle accidents and a statement about the ability of those granted motorcycle licenses to make decisions about their own welfare. These premises, however, are neither well reasoned nor sufficient to support the conclusion.

One of the largest flaws in the argument is that it relies on the assumption that the only reason for passing the helmet law is to prevent fatalities of motorcycle drivers. The author admits that helmets are instrumental in preventing "the type of fatalities associated with motorcycle accidents," yet he overlooks the additional benefits that could result from passing the helmet law. The author does not even discuss the kinds of injuries that can result from motorcycle accidents, such as paralysis and brain damage. Although these injuries are not fatal, they are certainly incapacitating and tragic. Laws such as Vermont's proposed helmet law not only prevent fatalities, but also result in lower incidence of these injuries.

Furthermore, the author states that only those older than 18 years of age can obtain a license to operate a motorcycle, and that 18-year olds are responsible enough for "making decisions about their own welfare." He fails to consider, however, what kinds of decisions these are. While 18-year olds may be considered adults legally, that alone does not guarantee they will make the rational decision to wear a motorcycle helmet. Additionally, there are already existing laws that override the individual's right to make decisions about his or her own welfare. Seatbelt laws, for example, mandate that every front-seat passenger in a moving vehicle is buckled in. This law is in effect in every state in the United States. So clearly, allowing 18-year olds to make their own decisions is not sufficient reason to oppose a helmet law.

The strongest argument against the author's point, however, is that preventing fatalities is reason enough to pass a helmet law. The author argues that "the majority of motorcycle accidents result in fatality only to the operator of the motorcycle," citing this as a reason to oppose the law, which is preposterous reasoning. While the operator of a motorcycle may nonchalantly take his life in his own hands, if permitted, by choosing not to wear a helmet, the state cannot permit such choices. The state has an obligation to protect the lives of its citizens, as is evidenced by the illegality of both murder and suicide. Any fatality that could have been prevented by the wearing of a motorcycle helmet is a senseless death; if proponents of the helmet law believe it will circumvent fatalities, that alone is reason enough for its passage.

The author might have strengthened his argument by citing fatality rates before and after the passage of similar laws in states other then Vermont. Had he demonstrated that the helmet law did not result in a lower incidence of fatality, his argument would have been more persuasive. But he did not; he chose to base his thesis on a flimsy assertion about 18-year olds making their own decisions and the fact that fatalities in motorcycle accidents are limited to the drivers of the motorcycles. The author's argument against the state of Vermont's proposed helmet law, therefore, is flawed and implausible, as it relies on a series of unsubstantiated premises and fallacious reasoning.

AWA Issue

The Analysis of an Issue essay asks you to choose a side on an issue and defend it. You may choose to side with either the proponents or opponents; each is equally valid.

The strongest essays of this type are:

Committed: Although you may enjoy playing devil's advocate in real life, on the GMAT you need to choose a side and stick to it. Arguing both for and against the issue will result in a weak essay and a lower score.

Supported: As you brainstorm, jot down three to five points in support of the side that you've chosen. As in the Analysis of an Argument, you'll take the strongest three of these and build your supporting paragraphs around them.

Specific: Come up with real-world examples to flesh out your supporting points. You can use examples from magazine articles you've read, experiences you've had, or common knowledge. Choose examples that can be adequately illustrated in the space and time available to you.

Thorough: Don't assume your readers share the same frame of reference as you. Explain any terms or allusions that are industry specific or technical. Your readers will be pleased you've made their job easier and will regard your essay more highly for its readability and educational content.

Let's work through writing an Analysis of the Issue argument that's based on the statement below.

> A prominent Wall Street analyst believes that only by catering to the tastes of the mainstream can a company be successful, and bases his investment strategies and advice on this belief. A well-known economist, however, argues that only by ensuring that specialized tastes and trends are encompassed can competition endure and the marketplace thrive.
>
> Which do you find more compelling: the analyst's position, or the economist's argument against it? Explain your position, using relevant reasons and/or examples drawn from your own experience, observations, or reading.

Brainstorming

First determine whether you agree with the analyst or the economist, then generate a list of reasons that support the side you've chosen to argue. Think of real-world examples to strengthen your position. Do your work here:

Whom do you agree with?

Why? (Reasons and examples)

The Format

The possible topics for this type of essay are endless, but they all follow similar patterns, and so should your essay. Again, stick to the five-paragraph persuasive essay format you learned in high school.

Introduction

Begin by briefly restating the argument and indicating which side you'll take (for or against). For example:

"Although many people believe that [summarize statement], there are many instances in which exactly the opposite is true. This essay will illustrate . . . ."

Supporting Paragraphs

Choose the three strongest points or examples from your brainstorming, and use each to develop a paragraph. Your paragraphs should be two to three sentences in length, and along the way you should make sure to let your reader know where you're heading with signpost words.

Another way to build an essay of this type is to illustrate ways in which the opposite position is flawed. Do not wander too far afield if you employ this tactic—choose one negative example and explore it.

Conclusion

Your concluding paragraph should be strong and clear. Recap your position and summarize your points, making use of conclusion words such as *as demonstrated above*, or *in conclusion*.

Go ahead and try writing an essay based on the Analysis of an Issue statement above, or read through our example of a well-written essay on this topic below. Pay attention to the format and the key words used throughout.

Our Sample

Although the prominent Wall Street analyst believes that "only by catering to the tastes of the mainstream can a company be successful," the economist's position that "only by ensuring that specialized tastes and trends are encompassed can competition endure" is more plausible. By illuminating the successes of three companies in the fashion industry, this essay will demonstrate that a company can be successful without catering to the mainstream.

The existence of different business models substantiates the argument that a company need not cater to the tastes of the mainstream in order to be successful and profitable. Hermes, the Italian leathergoods designers, has stood for the highest quality for several centuries. Had Hermes strayed from their identity in order to attempt to cater more to the mainstream, they would have clouded their purpose, confused their customers, and ultimately lost business. So companies whose business models dictate that they cater to super-exclusive or rarified tastes can and do succeed.

Second, it is important to remember that the very trends and styles that mainstream fashion designers popularize are actually borrowed from more avant-garde movements. The looks that grace the windows of every mall retailer this year were launched on high fashion runways last year, by what are in no way mainstream design houses. Without the influence of avant-garde fashion, trends would grow stale, popular retailers would have nothing new to sell to the mainstream, and the market would be less robust and competitive.

Finally, consider the case of America's most popular clothing retailer. The Gap was established as a clothing store whose mission was to sell well-made clothing staples, such as T-shirts and blue jeans. In the late 1980s, The Gap attempted to branch out into the retail clothing markets both above and below their demographic, selling both camouflage Army-style jackets and silk blouses. As consumers knew less what to expect from The Gap, sales plummeted. Only by returning to its original mission was The Gap able to recapture a substantial portion of its market. The Gap is now the number one clothing retailer in the United States, and they've captured this position by recommitting to their niche.

There are multiple examples of extremely successful companies that thrive in a competitive environment by focusing on a specific or exclusive niche of the market and ignoring the mainstream. Furthermore, companies secure in their niche, like The Gap, imperil their very success when they stray beyond their mission and try to cater to the mainstream. So we must conclude that the economist's position that "only by ensuring that specialized tastes and trends are encompassed can competition endure and the marketplace thrive" is ultimately more supportable.

STEP 8

GEOMETRY

The good news is that you probably won't encounter much geometry on the GMAT. The bad news is that the GMAT does test a wide base of fundamental geometry knowledge, most of which you learned in tenth grade and may have promptly forgotten. Who uses geometry on a daily basis, besides geometry teachers? To give you a better chance of acing any geometry problem you encounter, we're going to spend this chapter reviewing the main concepts and formulas.

LINES

A **line** is a set of points extending in two directions. When two lines intersect, they form angles.

ANGLES

The defining characteristic of **angles** is their measurement, or the number of degrees they contain. All angle measurements are relative to a circle, which, as you know, contains 360°. Half a circle is a 180° angle, which is also a straight line.

Angles come in three types: **acute** (smaller than 90°), **right** (equal to 90°), and **obtuse** (greater than 90°).

PARALLEL LINES

Two lines are considered **parallel** if they are the same distance from one another at all points, and therefore never meet. When parallel lines are crossed by a third line (that isn't perpendicular to them), two angles of different sizes are formed. For now, we'll call them big angles and little angles. All big angles have the same measurement in this situation, and all little angles also have the same measurement. The sum of any big angle and any little angle is 180°, because a big angle plus a little angle forms a line. In the diagram below, the measure of $\angle x = 145°$, $\angle x = \angle a$, and $\angle a + \angle b = 180°$.

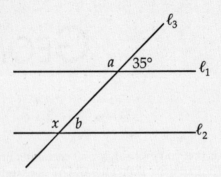

TRIANGLES

A closed, three-sided figure containing three angles is called a **triangle**.

HERE ARE A FEW FACTS YOU'LL NEED TO KNOW ABOUT TRIANGLES:

The sum of the measurement of all three angles inside a triangle is always 180°.

The largest angle in a triangle is always opposite the longest side.

The sum of the lengths of any two sides of a triangle is always greater than the length of the third.

Take a look at the diagram below:

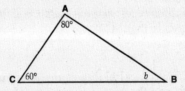

The measurement of angle b is 40°, because the sum of the other two angles is 140°.

$\overline{CB}$ is the longest side, because it is opposite the largest angle.

$\overline{AC} + \overline{AB} > \overline{BC}$; that is, the sum of the lengths of two sides (any two) is greater than the length of the third.

Triangles are defined by the sizes of their sides. A scalene triangle is one in which no two sides are equal, an isosceles triangle has two equal sides, and an equilateral triangle is one in which all three sides are of equal length. A right triangle is one that contains a right, or 90°, angle.

The Pythagorean Theorem

On the GMAT, questions about right triangles tend to center on one concept: the Pythagorean theorem.

The Pythagorean theorem can be used to determine the length of the sides of a right triangle. This theorem states that, in a right triangle, the square of the length of the longest side, or hypotenuse, is equal to the sum of the squares of the other two sides. Algebraically, the Pythagorean theorem is written $a^2 + b^2 = c^2$, where c is the hypotenuse.

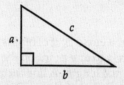

So in the right triangle above, if $a = 3$ and $c = 5$, can you determine the length of b? Start with the formula $a^2 + b^2 = c^2$ and substitute in the values you know.

$$3^2 + b^2 = 5^2$$

$$9 + b^2 = 25$$

$$b^2 = 25 - 9$$

$$b^2 = 16$$

$$b = 4$$

In fact, 3:4:5 is a commonly encountered right triangle on the GMAT, and if you are given two sides, you should automatically know the length of the third.

Now all you have left to learn about triangles are the formulas for perimeter and area. The perimeter of a triangle is the sum of the lengths of its sides, so for any triangle with sides of *a, b,* and *c,* the perimeter is expressed as $a + b + c$.

The **area** of any triangle is expressed by the formula $\frac{1}{2}bh$, where *b* is the length of the base and *h* is the height. The height is simply an imaginary perpendicular line drawn from the base of the triangle to its tallest point. Any side can be considered the base, as long as the line is drawn perpendicular.

QUADRILATERALS

Any four-sided figure is a **quadrilateral**. The main quadrilaterals you'll encounter on the GMAT are rectangles and squares.

A **rectangle** is a four-sided figure in which opposite sides are parallel and of equal length, and all angles are 90°. The perimeter of a rectangle is the sum of its sides, and the area is expressed as $A = lw$, where *l* is the length of one of the pairs of sides and *w* is the length of the other pair.

A **square** has four equal sides and four right angles. If *s* represents a side, then the perimeter of a square is 4s and its area is s².

CIRCLES

You probably know what a circle is; it contains 360°, and a line drawn from the center of the circle to any point on the circle is called its **radius**. All radii are of equal length. A line formed by two radii that cut across the center of the circle is called the **diameter**. An arc is any segment of the outside, or circumference of the circle.

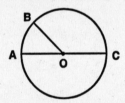

In the circle above, $\overline{OB}$ is a radius, $\overline{AC}$ is a diameter, and *AB* is an arc.

Two important formulas to memorize for circles you'll see on the GMAT are **circumference** (the distance around the circle) and **area**. Both formulas contain the constant π, or *pi*. You don't need to know the numerical value of π, just recognize that it is a little more than 3.

Circumference: $C = 2\pi r$ (*r* is the length of a radius)

Area: $A = \pi r^2$

So, in our circle above, if the radius $r = 3$, let's find the circumference and area.

Circumference:

$$C = 2\pi r$$

$$C = 2\pi(3)$$

$$C = 6\pi$$

Area:

$$A = \pi r^2$$

$$A = \pi(3)^2$$

$$A = 9\pi$$

You may see questions that only ask about a portion of a circle. For example, you may need to find the area of the shaded portion of the figure below, in which the measure of $\angle AOB = 90°$.

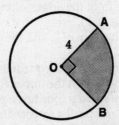

Start by looking at the angle at the center of the circle, and determine what fractional part of the circle it represents. The angle measures 90°, which is $\dfrac{1}{4}$ of 360°. So the shaded region is $\dfrac{1}{4}$ of the area of the circle. Since we know that the radius is 4, we know the area of the entire circle is 16π. $\dfrac{1}{4}$ of 16π is 4π, and that's the area of the shaded region.

COORDINATE GEOMETRY

Coordinate geometry, or Cartesian geometry is based on a grid formed by two number lines intersecting to form right angles. The horizontal line is called the x-axis, and the vertical line is called the y-axis. Their intersection is called the origin.

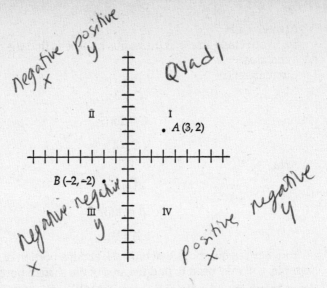

negative positive
x y

Quad 1

II

I

• A (3, 2)

B (-2, -2) •

negative negative
y
III

IV

positive negative
x y

Locations on the grid are called points or coordinate pairs, and are defined by their distance from the origin, along the x- and y-axes. So Point A on our diagram is $(3, 2)$, because the x-coordinate (the first one in the pair) is 3 units to the right of 0, and the y-coordinate (the second one) is 2 units up from 0.

Each quarter of the grid is called a quadrant. They are numbered counterclockwise, beginning with the upper right quadrant. So Quadrant I contains all positive x and y coordinate points $(+x, +y)$, Quadrant II contains all negative x and positive y coordinate points $(-x, +y)$, and so on. Point B on our diagram is located in Quadrant III, which contains all negative x- and y-coordinate points, and Quadrant IV contains all positive x-coordinate and negative y-coordinate points.

Every line in the coordinate grid can be expressed by the equation $y = mx + b$, which is commonly called the **slope formula**. Let's review what each variable stands for in this formula:

- y is the y-coordinate of a point.

- x is the x-coordinate of the same point.

- b is the y-intercept, or the y-coordinate of the point at which the line crosses the y-axis (when x is equal to zero).

- m is the **slope** of the line.

Slope is the ratio of the units the line runs vertically to the units the line runs horizontally. To find the slope of a line, you need to know two points on that line. The slope formula is $m = \frac{y_1 - y_2}{x_1 - x_2}$. Basically, you determine the slope of a line by subtracting one set of points from the other and setting the "rise" over the "run." So, for a line with points (6, 0) and (2, 3), here's how to find the slope:

$$\frac{y_1 - y_2}{x_1 - x_2} = \frac{0-3}{6-2} = -\frac{3}{4}$$

Now you know that for every 3 units the line runs across, it runs 4 up or down. The (–) tells us that the line runs down from left to right. Lines with positive slopes run up from left to right. ETS may use *a* instead of *m* to represent slope, but it means the same thing.

Okay, so back to our line, $y = mx + b$. If you know one point on the line and you know the slope, you can determine the y-intercept and plot the line on the coordinate grid. Suppose we are given the line $2x - 3y = 6$ and are asked for its y-intercept and slope. We simply need to rewrite the equation as $y = mx + b$, isolating y on one side of the equation.

$$2x - 3y = 6$$

$$-3y = 6 - 2x$$

$$3y = 2x - 6$$

$$y = \frac{2}{3}x - 2$$

So the slope of the line is $\frac{2}{3}$ and its y-intercept is –2.

$$y = \frac{2}{3}x - 2$$

slope.   y intercept

STEP 9

STATISTICS AND SPARE PARTS

Only a few topics remain for you to learn. They show up fairly infrequently on the GMAT, but you should still be prepared to face them. These topics include some basic statistics (very basic) and a hodge-podge of other pet topics of ETS's. You're most likely to see questions on the topics covered in this chapter if you are scoring above 600 overall.

FACTORIALS

At the end of our Formulas chapter, we discussed probabilities, which deals, for instance, with the likelihood of a certain event occurring. But ETS may ask you about the number of ways that you can combine events or things—for example, the number of ways 3 violinists, 2 cellists, and 4 bassists can be combined to form a trio of musicians. These types of manipulations are called combinations or permutations, depending on whether their order matters. We'll walk you through both, but first we need to teach you about factorials

A factorial looks like this: $x!$. The exclamation point means that you multiply the number by every positive integer less than the number. Yes, this is real math, but it's not that bad. Try it with 5:

$$5! = 5 \times 4 \times 3 \times 2 \times 1 = 120$$

You get the picture. Most of the time, you'll reduce the factorial before you multiply it out, so it won't get so messy that you'll need a calculator. Factorials are used to express the number of possibilities in problems dealing with combinations and permutations.

Combinations

Let's start with **combinations**, that is, counting the number of different ways a group of things can be combined.

> A dance team with five members will perform, two dancers at a time, until all the possible combinations of dancers have performed. If each combination dances for 5 minutes, and there are no breaks or interruptions, what is the total running time of the performance?
>
> ○   80 minutes
> ○   75 minutes
> ○   60 minutes
> ○   50 minutes
> ○   45 minutes

This is not as tough as it sounds. Here's the formula you need (memorize it):

$$C = \frac{n!}{r!(n-r)!}$$

n is the total number of things in the group and r is the number of things you're selecting. So in our problem about the dancers, $n = 5$ and $r = 2$.

The number of combinations of dancers, then, is

$$C = \frac{n!}{r!(n-r)!}$$

$$C = \frac{5!}{2!(5-2)!}$$

$$C = \frac{5!}{2!(3!)}$$

At this point, write out the factorials so you can start reducing:

$$C = \frac{5 \times 4 \times 3 \times 2 \times 1}{2 \times 1 (3 \times 2 \times 1)}$$

Notice that $3 \times 2 \times 1$ is on both the top and bottom, so you can reduce that part to 1. You're left with $C = \frac{5 \times 4}{2 \times 1}$, which reduces to $C = \frac{10}{1}$, or 10. So there are 10 combinations of dancers. If each performs for 5 minutes, the total performance time is 50 minutes, and the answer is (D).

Permutations

The problem above is one in which the order in which the dancers perform doesn't matter; you simply count the number of combinations. But when order does matter, the question is talking about a **permutation**.

> In a certain race, 5 contestants qualified for the finals. First, second, and third place will be awarded to 3 of these 5 contestants. How many different possible orders exist for the first, second, and third place winners?
>
> ○   5
> ○   20
> ○   60
> ○   90
> ○   120

To solve a permutation problem, use this formula (memorize this one too):

$$P = \frac{n!}{(n-r)}$$

n is the total number in the group you're drawing from, and r is the number of things you're arranging. So, in the problem above, $n = 5$ and $r = 3$.

$$P = \frac{n!}{(n-r)}$$

$$P = \frac{5!}{(5-3)!}$$

$$P = \frac{5!}{2!}$$

$$P = \frac{5 \times 4 \times 3 \times 2 \times 1}{2 \times 1}$$

Remember to reduce before you proceed. You're left with $P = 5 \times 4 \times 3$, or 60. There are 60 possible combinations of contestants, so the answer is choice (C).

FUNCTIONS

ETS may also try to confuse you with a question that looks like this:

If $p < q = \dfrac{p(p-q)}{q^2}$, then what is the value of $4 < 5$?

But don't worry. The little triangle is not some obscure symbol whose meaning you've forgotten. It's simply ETS's way of making a straightforward problem more complicated. Ignore the funky symbol and follow the directions you're given. Everywhere you see a p in the first equation, put a 4, and everywhere you see a q, replace it with 5. Then solve.

$$p < q = \frac{p(p-q)}{q^2}$$

$$4 < 5 = \frac{4(4-5)}{5^2}$$

$$= \frac{4(-1)}{25}, \text{ or}$$

$$-\frac{4}{25}$$

Easy enough, right?

SIMULTANEOUS EQUATIONS

Two or more equations that contain the same set of variables are called **simultaneous equations**. The cardinal rule of simultaneous equations is that, as long as you have the same number of equations as you have variables, you can solve for the variables. Therefore, solving for two variables requires two equations, three variables require three equations, and so on.

These appear most often in data sufficiency problems, and they look like this:

> What is the value of y?
> 1. $6x + 10y = 42$
> 2. $5x - 3y = 1$

or

> How many girls are in the chess club?
> 1. The chess club has a total of 50 members.
> 2. Twice the number of boys in the chess club is equal to three times the number of girls in the chess club.

You do not need to solve the equations. As long as you determine that you have two distinct equations and two of the same variables in each equation, you know that you need both statements together, and your answer is (C). A final note: This only works with <u>linear equations</u>, that is, <u>equations with no exponents</u>. If your simultaneous equations have exponents, you'll have to go ahead and work through them.

INEQUALITIES

First, let's review the symbols:

> $>$ means *greater than*
>
> $\geq$ means *greater than or equal to*

For instance, $5 > 3$ reads as 5 *is greater than* 3.

> $<$ means *less than*
>
> $\leq$ means *less than or equal to*

So $x \leq y$ reads x *is less than or equal to y*.

> $\neq$ means *is not equal to.*

So $x \neq 0$ means x *is not equal to* 0.

When you're working within equalities, you can manipulate and solve them just as you do equations, with one important exception. If you divide both sides by –1, or any multiple of –1, you have to reverse the inequality symbol.

Inequalities on the GMAT tend to present you with a range of values for your variables. For example:

> If $-6 \geq a \geq 12$ and $3 \leq b \leq 10$, which of the following represents the possible values of ab?
>
> ○ $-60 \leq ab \leq 120$
> ○ $-60 \leq ab \leq -18$
> ○ $-18 \leq ab \leq 36$
> ○ $-18 \leq ab \leq 120$
> ○ $36 \leq ab \leq 120$

To solve, plug in the greatest and least values for each variable. The least ab can equal is (-6×3) or -18, and the most ab can equal is (12×10) or 120, so the answer is $-18 \leq ab \leq 120$, or (D).

INTEREST

You've probably patronized banks for most of your life, but you may never have had to calculate interest on an account. Rest assured, it isn't as difficult as it might sound. There are two types of interest: simple and compound. We'll start with simple interest, because it's, well, more simple.

Take a look at the problem below:

— Simple
— compound

> If Andrew deposits $800 in a savings account that pays 3% interest annually, how much money will be in the account after one year?
>
> ○ $803
> ○ $816
> ○ $824
> ○ $832
> ○ $840

Simple interest is just a thinly disguised percentage problem, so translate:

What is 3% of $800?

$$x = \frac{3}{100} \cdot 800$$

$$x = 3 \times 8, \text{ or } 24$$

So Andrew's account gained $24 in one year, and his total savings are now $824. The answer is choice (C).

Compound interest comes up so rarely that you'll be fine if you Ballpark on problems dealing with it. In reality, compound interest usually yields just a little more than simple interest. This means that you can usually just compute the simple interest for the problem, and choose the next highest answer. Be careful, though—the simple interest will almost always be an answer choice, and it's a trap. —

STANDARD DEVIATION

It should not be surprising to you that ETS asks questions about bell curves. After all, the bell curve is their entire reason for being. You may have encountered bell curves in college—test grades in large classes are often given according to a bell curve.

Imagine that 100 students have taken a test. All the students' grades are plotted in a ratio to the average, or mean, score on the test. If their tests are graded according to a bell curve, this means that the number of A's is equal to the number of F's, the number of B's is equal to the number of D's, and a majority of the students get C's. Plotted on the curve, the grades would look like this:

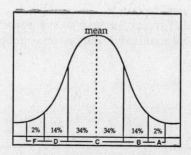

Two percent of the students gets A's, and 2% gets F's. Fourteen percent gets B's and D's, respectively, and 68% of the class receives a C. A graph of this type is considered a *normal distribution* and that's the only kind of distribution you'll see. This distribution represents the percentages for all normal bell curves. The percentages above and below the mean, 34, 14, and 2, are always the same. They represent a standard deviation from the mean. So the group of 34% above and the group of 34% below the mean is the first deviation, the two groups of 14% are the second deviation, and the two 2% groups are the third deviation. Together, all the deviations represent 100% of the group.

Deviations will be given as a number, and that number will tell you how far apart the values associated with the deviations are. Sketch out the graph, find the average, and add the deviation to find the values of each group.

Don't worry too much about what all this means. Just know how a bell curve works, and memorize the percentages (34, 14, and 2), and you'll be fine. Try this question for practice:

> The total weight of a group of fish is 2,800 pounds. If the weight of these fish has a normal distribution and the standard deviation equals 4 pounds, approximately how many of the fish weigh more than 32 pounds?
>
> ○ 14
> ○ 16
> ○ 34
> ○ 48
> ○ 50

To figure out the graph, start with the average. You know that the total weight of the fish is 2,800 pounds, and that there are 100 fish, so their average weight is 28 pounds.

Now jot down that average on your scratch paper, and make seven markings to represent standard deviations on your bell curve, like this:

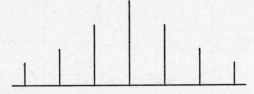

Label the middle one with your average, and fill in the percentages for each deviation.

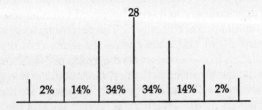

Now label each deviation. To do this, add the number you were given as the deviation to the number you found for your average. Your average is 28 and the deviation is 4 pounds, so the first deviation above the mean would be 32 pounds.

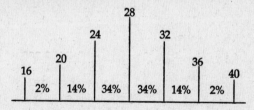

The question asks you how many of the fish weigh more than 32 pounds. That would be all the fish above the first deviation, and that's 16% of the fish (14% in the second deviation and 2% in the third). Sixteen percent of 100 fish is 16 fish, so the answer is choice (B).

STEP 10

THE FINAL STEP

THE NIGHT BEFORE

You're bound to be anxious the night before the GMAT. That's normal, but try not to freak out or stay up all night cramming. Here are a few things we recommend.

Getting It All Together

The night before, gather together everything you'll need on test day and put it in a sealed plastic bag or a shopping bag. Put that bag somewhere you won't forget it.

HERE'S A LIST OF THINGS YOU'LL NEED:

Your admissions ticket or confirmation numbers

Directions to the test center and the center's phone number

Several pencils with erasers or pens (your choice)

A light snack, like peanut butter crackers or an apple (steer clear of sugary foods)

A nonbeeping digital watch you know how to set

Some practice problems to warm up your brain

Remember your social security number - its your I.D.

Cram the Smart Way

We don't recommend you study much the night before the test. Instead, go get a massage, have a nice dinner out, or catch a light movie. If you feel like you must study, use your time wisely. To avoid becoming frustrated, review subject areas in which you're fairly confident. Don't revisit a problem that you've looked at six times and still don't understand—it will only raise your anxiety level. Instead, read through any notes you've made or review the techniques you've learned.

Don't Go Changing

Last of all, don't make any big changes in your life, especially the night before the test. If you normally go to bed at ten, go to bed at ten. If you usually eat a balanced breakfast or run five miles in the morning, do so on test day. There's no reason to disrupt your normal routine—you'll just feel disoriented and perform less than your best.

THE BIG DAY
At the Testing Center

Be sure to arrive at the testing center with time to spare. It's better to sit around in a lobby for 10 minutes than it is to rush in at the last minute, flustered and distracted. Use any extra time to work through some practice problems so your brain is warmed up when the test starts. When you arrive at the testing center the proctor will ask you to sign in, you'll put your valuables in a locker, and he or she will take a digital picture of you.

After this short prelude, you'll be escorted to your computer terminal. On the screen, you'll see your own picture and you'll be asked to confirm your name and social security number. Once you've done this, you won't need the keyboard, so you can shove it out of the way. On the desk you'll find scratch paper, a couple of pencils, a small lamp, and a set of earplugs. Go ahead and get comfortable.

Tutorial

Your testing experience will start with an onscreen tutorial, during which you'll be instructed on how to use a mouse, how to scroll, and other computer skills that you probably learned the first day you used a PC. The good news is that the tutorial is untimed, and that, unless your proctor strongly objects, you can use this time to write some A, B, C, D, Es on your scratch paper and jot down any formulas and step-by-step approaches you plan to use.

When you tell the computer you've had enough of the tutorial, your test will begin. Remember that you'll see the AWA essays first.

Focus and Move On

This is the real thing, so stay focused. When taking the test, there should be only two things on your mind: the problem in front of you and the time on the clock.

If you think you made a mistake on a problem you just finished, forget about it. There's nothing you can do about a problem once you've clicked *Answer Confirm*. Don't try to guess how well you're doing by assessing the difficulty of the problem in front of you—most people would guess incorrectly anyway. And even if you think you messed up the first section, give the second section everything you've got—you could be totally wrong about your performance.

Getting Your Score

When you've completed your last multiple-choice section, the computer may ask you to complete a marketing questionnaire. Read the instructions closely—you should know what you're getting into if you choose to proceed, and what you're missing (nothing) if you choose to skip it.

Finally, the computer will ask you whether or not you want to see your score. Of course you do. There is an option, however, called *Score Cancellation*. Canceling your score means that you will never, ever see the score for the test you just took, but your official score report will indicate that you cancelled your score.

You've done all this preparation—why on earth would you want to cancel your score? Unless you became violently ill during the test, or the test center's roof was lifted off by a tornado during your testing time, do not cancel your score. You probably did fine, and if you didn't quite hit your target score, you can retest in the next calendar month.

Since you want to see your score, tell the computer that. It will ask you again (*Are you sure?*) but don't be paranoid. It's just double checking. Your score will be displayed on the screen, and only on the screen. Be sure to write your score on a piece of scratch paper, as your proctor may not be able to retrieve it once you leave the computer terminal.

PART **III**

THE DRILLS

VERBAL DRILLS

SENTENCE CORRECTION DRILL

1. <u>Unlike the United States, where the head of state is chosen in a popular election separate from that which determines the majority party of the legislative branch, the Prime Minister of India</u> is elected by the members of the majority party of Parliament.

   ○ Unlike the United States, where the head of state is chosen in a popular election separate from that which determines the majority party of the legislative branch, the Prime Minister of India

   ○ Unlike the United States, in which the head of state is chosen in a popular election separate from that which determines the majority party of the legislative branch, the Prime Minister of India

   ○ Unlike that of the United States, where a popular election separate from that which determines the majority party of the legislative branch chooses the head of state, India has a Prime Minister that

   ○ In comparison with the United States, where a popular election separate from that which determines the majority party of the legislative branch chooses the head of state, the Prime Minister of India

   ○ In the United States, the head of state is chosen in a popular election separate from that which determines the majority party of the legislative branch, but in India the Prime Minister

2. While five years ago, only 10 percent of women said they kept a handgun for home security, today that figure is 35 percent, making handguns the most popular type of home security for women <u>as well as men</u>.

○ as well as men
○ as well as for men
○ and men too
○ and men as well
○ and also men

3. Even though the Mt. Everest team began the expedition with more provisions than <u>they had in any previous year</u>, its food lasted through only the first twelve days of the climb.

○ they had in any previous year
○ their previous years had had
○ they had for any previous year
○ in their previous years
○ it had in any previous year

4. <u>With their similar price ranges and menus, "theme" restaurants located in shopping malls often succeed despite the fact that they are clustered next to one another; one reason is suggested by the behavior of their customers, who would rather eat in proximity to the area in which they are shopping than leave the area to eat, even if this means choosing from limited options.</u>

○ With their similar price ranges and menus, "theme" restaurants located in shopping malls often succeed despite the fact that they are clustered next to one another; one reason is suggested by the behavior of their customers, who would rather eat in proximity to the area in which they are shopping than leave the area to eat, even if this means choosing from limited options.

○ If clustered next to each other in shopping malls, one reason that "theme" restaurants with similar price ranges and menus succeed is suggested by the behavior of their customers, who would rather eat in the area in which they are shopping than leave the area to eat, even if this means choosing from limited options.

○ If clustered next to each other in shopping malls, one reason that "theme" restaurants with similar price ranges and menus succeed is suggested by their customers, who would rather eat in proximity to the area in which they are shopping even if this means choosing from limited options than those who would rather leave the area to eat.

○ The fact that there are customers who would rather eat in the area in which they are shopping even if this means choosing from limited options than leave the area to eat is suggestive of one reason, if clustered next to one another in shopping malls, "theme" restaurants with similar price ranges and menus can succeed.

○ The fact that there are customers who would rather eat in the area in which they are shopping than leave the area to eat suggests one reason "theme" restaurants with similar price ranges and menus located in shopping malls can succeed despite being clustered next to one another.

5. Many economic analysts believe that a substantial increase in the number of nonprofessionals using online trading services should lead to <u>raising the overall volume of the market, as well as lowering fears about investing</u>, and a surge in public confidence in the economy.

- ○ raising the overall volume of the market, as well as lowering fears about investing
- ○ a raising of the overall volume of the market, a lowering of fears about investing
- ○ a raising of the overall volume of the market, along with lowering fears about investing
- ○ the overall volume of the market being raised, along with fears about investing being lowered
- ○ the overall volume of the market raising, and fears about investing lowering

6. In the latter years of The Great Depression, colleagues of Franklin <u>Roosevelt's argued that his proposed Social Security Act has</u> a good chance of succeeding due to its strong bipartisan support, sound fiscal plan, and widespread electoral approval.

- ○ Roosevelt's argued that his proposed Social Security Act has
- ○ Roosevelt's argued that his proposed Social Security Act had
- ○ Roosevelt's have argued that his proposed Social Security Act had
- ○ Roosevelt argued that his proposed Social
- ○ Roosevelt had argued that his proposed Social Security Act has

7. <u>From 1995 to 1998 the average daily retail sales of women's apparel increased between 12 and 16 percent annually.</u>

- ○ From 1995 to 1998 the average daily retail sales of women's apparel increased between 12 and 16 percent annually.

○ Twelve to sixteen percent is the annual increase in the average daily retail sales of women's apparel in the years 1995 to 1998.

○ The average daily retail sales of women's apparel have increased annually 12 and 16 percent in the years 1995 to 1998.

○ Annually an increase from 12 to 16 percent has occurred between 1995 and 1998 in the average daily retail sales of women's apparel.

○ Occurring from 1995 to 1998 was an annual increase of 12 to 16 percent in the average daily retail sales of women's apparel.

8. An uncommon method of home building relies on the construction of extremely thick walls to reduce the energy needs due to heating and cooling; the resulting building, with <u>internal spaces that maintain a constant temperature although the outside air that flows through them varies in temperature, are known as "earth ships."</u>

○ internal spaces that maintain a constant temperature although the outside air that flows through them varies in temperature, are known as "earth ships."

○ internal spaces that maintain a constant temperature although they are supplied by varying temperatures of outside air, are known as "earth ships."

○ internal spaces that maintain a constant temperature although the outside air that flows through them varies in temperature, is known as an "earth ship."

○ constant temperature internal spaces although the outside air that flows through them varies in temperature, are known as "earth ships."

○ internal spaces that maintain a constant temperature although they are supplied by varying temperatures of outside air, is known as an "earth ship."

9. In most major metropolitan areas, the number of hate crimes per capita is significantly lower in neighborhoods in which the population is racially mixed, <u>that is, no more than one-third of the area's inhabitants belong to the same ethnic group; it is theorized that a person is less likely to commit a hate crime against someone who he regards as a neighbor.</u>

- ○ that is, no more than one-third of the area's inhabitants belong to the same ethnic group; it is theorized that a person is less likely to commit a hate crime against someone who he regards as a neighbor

- ○ that is, no more than one-third of the area's inhabitants belong to the same ethnic group; it is theorized that a person is less likely to commit a hate crime against someone whom he regards as a neighbor

- ○ that is, no more than one-third of the area's inhabitants belongs to the same ethnic group; it is theorized that a person is less likely to commit a hate crime against someone whom he regards as a neighbor

- ○ that is, no more than one-third of the area's inhabitants belongs to the same ethnic group; it is theorized that a person is less likely to commit a hate crime against someone who he regards as a neighbor

- ○ that is, no more than one-third of the area's inhabitants belongs to the same ethnic group; it is theorized that a person is less likely to commit a hate crime against someone whom he regards to be a neighbor

10. <u>Each of Henry VIII's six wives—excluding Jane Seymour, who died in childbirth, and Katherine Parr, who outlived him—were either divorced by Henry or executed by the state.</u>

○ Each of Henry VIII's six wives—excluding Jane Seymour, who died in childbirth, and Katherine Parr, who outlived him—were either divorced by Henry or executed by the state.

○ Excluding Jane Seymour, who died in childbirth, and Katherine Parr, who outlived him, each of Henry VIII's six wives were either divorced by Henry or executed by the state.

○ With the exception of Jane Seymour, who died in childbirth, and Katherine Parr, who outlived him, every one of Henry VIII's six wives were either divorced by Henry or executed by the state.

○ Each of Henry VIII's six wives—excluding Jane Seymour, who died in childbirth, and Katherine Parr, who outlived him—was either divorced by Henry or executed by the state.

○ Divorced by Henry VIII or executed by the state were each of Henry VIII's six wives, excluding Jane Seymour, who died in childbirth, and Katherine Parr, who outlived him.

Sentence Correction Drill Answer Key

1.	E	6.	D	
2.	B	7.	A	
3.	E	8.	C	
4.	A	9.	C	
5.	B	10.	D	

Sentence Correction Drill Answers and Explanations

1. **E** Did you find the error in the sentence? It contains a parallel construction error. The sentence compares *the United States* to *the Prime Minister*. A secondary error is the misuse of *where*. Remember, *where* is for physical locations only.

   (A) No. The sentence contains an error, so get rid of this answer choice, as it is always identical to the underlined portion of the sentence.

   (B) No. This answer choice compares *the United States* to *the Prime Minister*.

   (C) No. This choice is not parallel—it compares *that of the United States* to *India*.

   (D) No. This answer choice compares *the United States* to *the Prime Minister*. Furthermore, it uses the word *where* instead of *in which*.

   (E) Yes. The stem sentence's problem is fixed, because the sentence parallels *in the United States* with *in India*. Additionally, the misuse of *where* is corrected.

2. **B** This sentence contains a comparison that's not parallel. The correct construction is *for women as well as for men*.

   (A) No. This is not parallel. Handguns are the most popular *for women*, and so they should be the most popular *for men*, too.

   (B) Yes. This sentence contains the correct idiom *as well as* and uses parallel construction to compare how popular handguns are *for women* and *for men*.

   (C) No. This choice is not parallel, and *and . . . too* is redundant.

   (D) No. This is not parallel. Also, *and . . . as well* is redundant.

   (E) No. This is not parallel, and *and also* is redundant.

3. **E**   This sentence contains a pronoun error. *Team* is singular, so the underlined portion should read *it had* . . . All but one of the answer choices repeat the error.

(A) No. *Team* is singular, so the pronoun should be *it*, not *they*.

(B) No. *Team* is singular, so the pronoun should be *it*, not *their*. Also, this choice makes it sound as though the years had provisions.

(C) No. This contains the same pronoun error as the original sentence: *team* is singular, so the pronoun should be *it*, not *they*.

(D) No. Pronoun error again—*Team* is singular, so the pronoun should be *it*, not *their*.

(E) Yes. This answer choice fixes the stem's pronoun problem by replacing the plural *they* with a singular *it*.

4. **A**   This is a long sentence, but it has no apparent errors. Since you could not spot the error in the underlined portion of the sentence, you should have gone to each answer choice, and when you found an error there, eliminated it.

(A) Yes. This answer choice is long and a bit clunky, but it doesn't violate any rules.

(B) No. As written, the sentence says that *one reason* is *clustered next to each other*, which is a misplaced modifier.

(C) No. This choice contains the same misplaced modifier as (B). *Suggested by their customers* is another error—it is their behavior that suggests, not the customers themselves.

(D) No. Although it appears at the end of the sentence rather than the beginning, *one reason* is modified by *if clustered next to each other*, which doesn't make sense. Furthermore, the sentence's subject, *the fact*, does not make sense with the sentence's verb, *is suggestive*. It is not the fact that is suggestive, but the customers' behavior.

(E) No. *The fact* does not suggest one reason the restaurants can succeed. Instead, consumers' behavior suggests one reason the restaurants can succeed. Also, the phrase *menus located in shopping malls* makes it sound as though the menus, rather than the restaurants, are located in shopping malls. And remember, ETS hates *being*.

5. **B**   This sentence contains a list—*raising, lowering,* and *a surge*—so you should expect an error in parallel construction. All the parts of the list must be the same part of speech for the list to be parallel. Since *a surge* is not underlined, you will need to find an answer choice that changes *raising* and *lowering* to nouns to match *a surge.*

(A) No. Look for parallel construction. The other list item is *a surge* so we need *a raising* and *a lowering.*

(B) Yes. This choice fixes the stem's parallel construction problem. The other list items are now *a raising, a lowering,* and *a surge.*

(C) No. Although this choice fixes the stem's incorrect *raising* by making it *a raising,* it introduces a nonparallel phrase: *along with lowering fears about investing.*

(D) No. This is not parallel—the nonunderlined portion of the sentence contains *a surge,* which is a noun, so we need nouns in the underlined portion of the list. Also, don't forget that ETS hates *being.*

(E) No. We know ETS hates *being,* so we should eliminate this answer choice. It isn't parallel either. The other list item is *a surge* so we need *a raising* and *a lowering.* Also, for you grammar buffs, raising and lowering are transitive verbs, so they need a direct object (something that's raised or lowered).

6. **D**   This sentence contains a verb tense error. When an event occurred in the past and is over, we use the simple past tense; in this case, *Act had a good chance of succeeding.* Look at the ends of the answer choices for the two-thirds split that allows you to eliminate (A) and (E) right away. The sentence also contains an error in the use of the possessive: *colleagues of . . . Roosevelt's* is redundant. The correct usage is either *colleagues of . . . Roosevelt* or *Roosevelt's colleagues.*

(A) No. This happened in the past, so *has* is wrong. Also, the possessive on *Roosevelt's* is redundant.

(B) No. *Roosevelt's* is redundant.

(C) No. *Roosevelt's* is redundant, and the verb tense in *have argued* is incorrect. The arguing occurred in the past, concluded in the past, and is not linked to any other event, so the verb should be simple past, *argued.*

(D) Yes. This answer choice corrects the stem's incorrect *of . . . Roosevelt's*. Also, the two verbs are both in the simple past tense.

(E) No. This choice has a verb tense error. This obviously happened in the past, yet the verb given here is the present tense *has*.

7. **A**   If you don't see an error in the original sentence, go to Plan B—examine each of the answer choices to find an error and eliminate it.

(A) Yes. This is direct and to the point. There is no error.

(B) No. This is a verb tense error. We are dealing with the past, so the increase *was* 12 to 16 percent, not *is*.

(C) No. The years are in the past, so it's incorrect to say that the average daily retail sales *have* increased. We need the simple past tense; *increased*. Also, the idiom is used incorrectly—the increase should be expressed as *between 12 and 16 percent* or as *12 to 16 percent*.

(D) No. This is the incorrect verb tense. We are dealing with the past, so it's incorrect to say that the increase *has* occurred.

(E) No. It is too awkward to make the increase the subject of the sentence. The subject should be *sales*, and *increase* should be what happened to the sales.

8. **C**   This sentence contains a problem in subject/verb agreement. The subject, *building* is singular, so it needs a singular verb, *is known*. This error is in the 2/3 split, so you can eliminate (A), (B), and (D).

(A) No. The verb should be *is known as*.

(B) No. This contains the same subject/verb agreement error as (A). Eliminate it.

(C) Yes. A little clunky, but this choice fixes the stem's subject/verb problem.

(D) No. This choice contains the original error of *are known*. Also, the first four words of this choice are very awkward. *Temperature* should not be used as an adjective to describe *spaces*.

(E) No. This choice changes the meaning of the sentence. The interval spaces are not *supplied* with *temperatures*. Air flows through them. Eliminate this answer choice.

9. **C** The underlined portion of this sentence contains two errors: a subject/verb disagreement, and a misused pronoun. The subject of the clause is *one-third*, which is singular, so it requires the singular verb, *belongs*. *Who* should be *whom*. If you have trouble determining whether to use *who* or *whom*, restate the sentence substituting *he* or *him* for *who* or *whom*. In this sentence, *someone regards **him** as a neighbor*—since it's *him*, use *whom*. These two errors should allow you to quickly eliminate answer choices that contain one or both of them.

(A) No. *Belong* should be *belongs* to agree with *one-third* and *who* should be *whom*.

(B) No. This choice corrects the pronoun misuse but does not fix the subject/verb disagreement in *belong*.

(C) Yes. This choice uses the correct verb *belongs* and the correct pronoun *whom*.

(D) No. *Belongs* is correct, but *who* is not.

(E) No. Although this choice corrects the subject/verb disagreement and the pronoun misuse, it introduces a new error, *regards . . . to be*. The correct idiomatic expression is *regards . . . as*.

10. **D** This sentence contains a subject/verb disagreement. *Each* is short for *each one* and is singular, so it calls for the singular verb *was*. You will quickly eliminate most of the answer choices if you focus on this error.

(A) No. This choice has an error in subject/verb agreement. *Each* is singular and needs a singular verb.

(B) No. Rearranging the sentence does not get rid of the subject/verb disagreement. The verb still needs to be *was* in order to agree with the subject *each*.

(C) No. Changing *each* to *every one* does not help. *Every one* is singular and needs the singular verb *was*.

(D) Yes. This choice is nearly identical to the original sentence except that it uses the correct verb *was*.

(E) No. The subject is still *each*, the verb is still *were*, and the sentence is still wrong. Plus, radically rearranging the sentence is rarely the solution to the grammar errors you'll see on the GMAT.

1. *A researcher concluded her report on a study testing a new antihypertension drug by saying, "Patients who used the new drug have experienced no significant side effects." The editor of the medical journal to which she submitted the report suggested that she change the conclusion to "Patients who used the new drug appear thus far to have experienced no significant side effects."*

    Which of the following, if true, provides the best logical justification for the editor's suggestion that the researcher's conclusion be altered?

    ○ Some patients who took the new antihypertension drug experienced a mild increase in nausea, a side effect easily averted by taking the medication with food.

    ○ The new antihypertension drug could have caused side effects, the visible signs of which have not yet appeared in the patients who participated in the study.

    ○ The researcher's report does not sufficiently compare the effects of the antihypertension drug with those of other, established antihypertension drugs.

    ○ The majority of Americans have blood pressure far enough outside the "normal" range to be considered at least mildly hypertensive.

    ○ The severity of side effects from antihypertension drugs varies from patient to patient.

2. *The World Bank has developed a computer program that assesses the authenticity of world currency suspected of being counterfeit. The program contains extensive profiles of the printing techniques and components of currencies of all major nations; such profiles include chemical composition of paper, density of ink, and details in the printing plates that are invisible to the naked eye. Counterfeiters, including the best counterfeiters known from history, cannot hope to reproduce all facets of a particular nation's currency.*

   Which of the following can be logically concluded from the passage above?

   ○ The staff resources required to prepare currency for analysis by the program make use of the program prohibitively expensive.

   ○ Consumer banks will soon purchase the right to use the program on their own computers.

   ○ The program cannot fail to identify as inauthentic counterfeit currency that has previously escaped detection.

   ○ The authentication program has taken a number of years to develop.

   In numerous cases, authentic currency is not recognized as authentic by the program.

3. **Director of Foreign Language School:** *We should stop giving our students the* La Langue Facile *tape series and begin to distribute the* Les Bons Mots *series instead.*

   Assistant Director: *Why?*

   Director: *Because it takes 31 percent more time for teachers to prepare lessons using the* La Langue Facile *tape series than it takes for teachers to prepare lessons using the* Les Bons Mots *tape series. This time would be better spent working directly with students.*

Assistant Director: *That is not a sufficient reason to change instructional tapes. We can simply hire teachers who already have planned lessons based on the* La Langue Facile *tape series*.

Which of the following, if true, most seriously undermines the assistant director's objection to the argument made by the director?

○ All teachers in the school district are currently required to attend classes to learn how to adapt the *La Langue Facile* tapes to new educational standards.

○ Once teachers have made lesson plans, they are more willing to move from their current positions to positions with new language schools.

○ Teachers with established lesson plans hired by foreign language schools are required to put in additional hours in administrative support, hours equal to the time they would have spent in making lesson plans.

○ The average improvement in scores on tests of fluency in the director's school is below the average improvement in standardized test scores in otherwise comparable schools.

○ The supplemental course materials required for use with the *Les Bons Mots* tape series require teachers to invest a great deal of time in logistical arrangements, such as arranging for videocassette recorders and photocopying quizzes.

4. An automobile manufacturer's engineering
    department developed a new model of its best-
    selling sedan that lacked certain safety features
    present in the earlier model, which was still being
    produced. During the first year of production of
    the new model, while both models were being
    sold, the newer model of the sedan sold much
    better than the older model. The CEO of the
    automobile company concluded that safety
    features were not important in consumers'
    decisions to purchase the sedan.

    Which of the following, if true, would most
    seriously weaken the CEO's conclusion?

    ○   The automobile company sells cars both
        for inclusion in corporate fleets and for
        individual use.

    ○   Many customers consider the new sedan
        safe because of certain features in its
        steering mechanism and body style.

    ○   Many of those who purchased the new
        sedan also own another car manufactured
        by the same automobile company.

    ○   The new sedan has sold to more custom-
        ers in the 18-to-25 age bracket.

    ○   There was no significant difference in
        price between the newer sedan and the
        older model.

5. A new company can offer stocks in an initial public
    offering (IPO) before the company has proven itself
    capable of generating long-term profits for its
    stockholders. Historically, if a company has seemed
    likely to generate profits, the stock price in the IPO
    has risen; if the company seemed less likely to
    generate profits, the stock price in the IPO has
    fallen. Today business analysts announced that the
    Tenon Corporation has turned a profit in the
    financial quarter just completed. Therefore, stock
    prices for the Tenon Corporation's IPO, which is
    planned for next week, will rise.

    The author's conclusion about Tenon Corporation
    is based on faulty reasoning because it

- O depends on the assumption that what has been true in the past will hold true in the future.
- O relies on a line of reasoning that is circular.
- O confuses cause with effect.
- O overlooks cases in which the counterexample is true.
- O rests on a faulty comparison.

6. *A company that disposes of industrial waste employs dozens of people in jobs that are considered quite hazardous. The company obeys federal regulations governing workplace safety, and, to comply with new regulations instituted to avoid recently discovered risks from airborne particulate matter, company engineers were required to install extremely expensive air-filtering equipment. However, despite the expense of the air-filtering equipment, the company's operating costs for the quarter were considerably lower than normal.*

    Which of the following, if true, most helps to resolve the apparent paradox?

- O More than half the company's expenditures to maintain worker safety go to pay for protective garments, yet only a small percentage of such expenditures go to pay for nose and mouth filters.
- O Expensive shutdowns to prevent contamination that were periodically required prior to the installation of the air-filtering equipment are no longer necessary.
- O The company's costs of labor, which make up a large fraction of operating costs, increased during the same period.
- O When the air-filtering equipment was installed in the waste disposal facility, the company took the opportunity to upgrade the temperature control equipment.
- O The majority of the company's employees work in the areas of the plant in which the air-filtering equipment was installed.

7. *The diamond mines of Extopia produced so many diamonds that the market was overwhelmed; consumption did not keep pace with production. As a result, diamond prices fell. The government of Extopia attempted to support diamond prices through a subsidy scheme: Diamond producers who voluntarily limited the number of diamonds they produced were compensated directly by the government up to a specified maximum payment.*

The program instituted by the government of Extopia, if successful, will not result in a net cost increase to the government. Which of the following, if true, is the best basis for an explanation of how this could be true?

○ Depressed diamond prices meant operating losses for diamond producers, decreasing the income of diamond producers, and thus decreasing the taxes paid to the government by diamond producers.

○ Diamond production in countries other than Extopia declined in the same year Extopia's government instituted the compensatory scheme.

○ In the first quarter after Extopia's government instituted the compensatory scheme, diamond production declined 8 percent.

○ Because the government specified a maximum subsidy payment per diamond producer, those producers with numerous mines in operation received less support per mine than those producers with fewer mines in operation.

○ Diamond producers desiring to qualify for the compensatory scheme could not continue to produce diamonds and simply withhold them from the market.

8. *Pharmaceutical companies typically charge slightly inflated prices for drugs that have a large customer base and are heavily prescribed by doctors, in order to balance the losses such companies experience from producing "orphan" drugs—drugs that are used by so few patients that they can never be profitable. New federal regulations require pharmaceutical companies to limit the price they charge for any drug to cost plus a predetermined percentage profit.*

If the statements above are true, which of the following must also be true?

○ New pharmaceutical technology has made advances possible; the drugs produced by such technology, however, are too expensive for all but the wealthiest patients.

○ If pharmaceutical companies do not find another source of income to balance the losses they experience in producing orphan drugs, such companies will no longer be able to produce those drugs without compromising overall profits.

○ Some patients already request generic pharmaceuticals, when they are available, because they are typically less expensive than name-brand pharmaceuticals.

○ If pharmaceutical companies reduce the costs of producing most drugs, they will be able to earn more profits despite the new law, and thus will be able to balance the losses they experience from the production of orphan drugs.

○ Even though charitable organizations that fund research into the rare diseases treated by orphan drugs provide some donations to offset the costs of the drugs, such donations are declining.

9. *Gas leaks are a danger for households in which certain standards of safety are not maintained. So that householders are able to detect such hazards before they become serious enough to pose a danger, the county fire safety board has mailed a newsletter to all residents of the county, listing ways to detect a gas leak and encouraging householders to check for such signs.*

Which of the following, if true, is the best criticism of the newsletter as a means of achieving the fire safety board's goals?

○ Many gas leaks have certain warning signs that cannot be detected during an investigation by a householder.

○ Once a gas leak is known to exist, the steps taken to eliminate such a hazard vary according to the type and location of the leak.

○ The newsletter was sent to all residents of the county, including those who maintain the standards of safety that preclude the possibility of a gas leak.

○ Gas leaks are more common in single-family homes than they are in apartments.

○ People who do not maintain minimal standards of safety are unlikely to inspect their homes for the signs of gas leaks.

10. *Women make up a larger proportion of workers in the information services industry than they did ten years ago. In 1985, only 7 percent of women in the workforce were employed in the information services industry, but in 1995, more than 16 percent of women in the workforce were employed in the information services industry.*

To evaluate the truth of the argument above, it would be most useful to compare 1985 and 1995 with regard to which of the following characteristics?

○ the percentage of women in the workforce who were not employed in the information services industry

○ the percentage of women who are now retired, and who have formerly worked in the information services industry

○ the percentage of women who have been promoted to managerial positions within the information services industry

○ the percentage of men in the workforce who were employed in the information services industry

○ the percentage of men who will soon be eligible for employment in the information services industry

Arguments Drill Answer Key

1.	B	6.	B
2.	C	7.	A
3.	C	8.	B
4.	B	9.	E
5.	A	10.	D

Argument Drill Answers and Explanations

1. **B** This argument asks you to support the editor's position, which hinges around her statement, *thus far*. Her point is that there may be patients who have taken the new drug and who have not yet shown side effects, but may in the future. She assumes that there are such patients, and the fact that patients have not shown side effects yet does not mean there aren't any. A good answer choice here will clearly establish that difference.

    (A) No. You may have been tempted to pick this because it gives a side effect. However, this answer choice contradicts the editor's statement, in which no significant side effects are reported.

    (B) Yes. The key in the editor's statement is *thus far*, which implies that side effects could still show up in the future, and this answer choice addresses that possibility.

    (C) No. This is out of scope. The editor doesn't care about comparing this drug to others, just whether there are side effects of this drug.

    (D) No. This is out of scope. We don't really care about the general state of hypertension in the United States.

    (E) No. Both individual side effects and all hypertension drugs are out of scope.

2. **C** This is an Inference question, so we need an answer choice we know to be true from the argument. All we know about is the ability of one particular computer program to detect counterfeit currency, and how it does so.

    (A) No. We have no idea how expensive the program is, and "prohibitively" is extreme.

    (B) No. Possibly, but nothing in the argument talks about consumer banks, so this is out of scope.

(C) Yes. This must be true. The passage says that the program looks at printing techniques and that even the best counterfeiters cannot hope to have replicated all aspects of these techniques. Therefore, the program will detect all counterfeits.

(D) No. This may be true, but the information in the passage doesn't tell us how long development of the program took.

(E) No. This appears nowhere in the passage, and in fact contradicts the argument that this program works very well.

3. **C** We need to attack the assistant director's argument. He proposes to hire teachers who have *La Langue Facile* lesson plans instead of changing to a less time-intensive instructional tape series. If we can show that his plan would not have the desired result of allowing teachers to spend more time with their students, we will have weakened his argument.

(A) No. Class requirements and new educational standards are out of scope.

(B) No. If anything, this answer choice would strengthen the assistant director's argument, because it indicates that his plan may be somewhat easy to implement.

(C) Yes. The assistant director wants to hire teachers who already have *La Langue Facile* lesson plans because he assumes they will have more time to spend with students. But here we find out that those teachers will just have to use that lesson-planning time somewhere else. This weakens the assistant director's argument.

(D) No. Fluency test scores and students' performance are out of scope.

(E) No. This just tells us why switching to *Les Bons Mots* may not save time. Be careful. This answer choice weakens the *director's* point of view, not the assistant director's.

4. **B** Here we want to know about safety features, and whether they're important to buyers. To weaken the CEO's conclusion that safety features were not important, we need to show that consumers did consider safety to be important, or show another explanation for the consumers' decision.

(A) No. This is out of scope. We don't care who the buyers are; we only need to weaken the idea that safety features weren't important to those buyers.

(B) Yes. We have evidence that safety features are important to buyers, it's just that the buyers have a different opinion of what makes a vehicle safe.

(C) No. This doesn't explain the difference between this company's old and new models' performance.

(D) No. It doesn't matter to what age groups the car appeals. This is out of scope.

(E) No. Knowing that the price is the same does not help us weaken the argument. If we had learned the new model was cheaper, however, we would have had an alternate cause for the sales results, which would have been a good way to weaken the argument.

5. **A** This is a Reasoning question, so pay attention to how the author constructs his argument. He takes a historical trend and uses it to predict the outcome of a specific event. As you read through the answer choices, simply ask yourself, "Did he do that?"

(A) Yes. The author based his conclusion about Tenon on the assumption that what has been true in the past (in an IPO, a company that seemed likely to generate profits saw an increase in their stock price) will be true for Tenon.

(B) No. There is no circular reasoning here.

(C) No. There is no confusion of cause and effect—potential profits cause an increase in stock price.

(D) No. There are no counterexamples given, so this answer choice is out of scope.

(E) No. There is no comparison made in the argument, so this cannot be the credited response.

6. **B** Resolve the Paradox: How can operating costs be lower when the new equipment is so expensive?

(A) No. This is out of scope. We are concerned with air-filtering equipment, not garments or facial filters.

(B) Yes. Here we are given an explanation of how operating costs could go down (the shutdowns, with their expense, are eliminated) even as the new equipment is present. The equipment actually forestalls additional costs.

(C) No. This tells us that operating costs went up, not how they went down.

(D) No. This answer choice also tells us about how operating costs went up, not how they went down.

(E) No. Though this answer choice does give some details about the new equipment, it doesn't tell us why operating costs could have gone down.

7. A Resolve the Paradox: How can the government subsidize diamond producers and still not experience an increase in net cost? (Note that the second part of the paradox is in the question, not in the argument.)

(A) Yes. Here we find out that the government collected less in taxes from diamond producers when prices were bad. Paying subsidies would make up for the operating losses, increase diamond producers' income, and increase taxes to the government, which would compensate for the subsidies.

(B) No. This doesn't help. If diamond production in other countries declined, then prices for diamonds would increase overall and the program would be unnecessary.

(C) No. This answer choice tells us the goal of the program is satisfied, but it doesn't tell us anything about the cost to the government. It only speaks to one side of the paradox.

(D) No. This answer choice doesn't talk about the overall effect that the subsidies would have on the government.

(E) No. This is irrelevant. The rules imposed on the diamond producers won't change the money the government pays them, and that's the issue we're interested in.

8. B This is an Inference, so the correct answer will be something you know from the argument.

(A) No. We have no information about the drugs' cost to the patient.

(B) Yes. If the companies can no longer place surcharges on more popular drugs, they will lose the sources of revenue that balance the losses from orphan drugs. They will have to find other revenue sources, or lose money.

(C) No. The passage provides no information about generic drugs—it's out of scope.

(D) No. This is contradicted by the argument, which says there will be a constant percentage of profit allowed. So if drug costs are reduced, the profit should be commensurately reduced.

(E) No. There is no information in this argument about charitable organizations and offsetting of costs.

9. **E** This is a Weaken question, and so we need to attack the author's assumption that the newsletter will cause early detection of gas leak hazards. Since his assumption is a causal one, the best attack will either show that the newsletter will not cause early detection of gas leaks, or that something else will cause early detection of gas leaks, so the newsletter is not necessary.

(A) No. The nondetectable signs of gas leaks are out of scope. We are concerned only with the detectable warning signs of a gas leak.

(B) No. This answer choice focuses on what happens after detection, so it's out of scope. We're interested only in detection.

(C) No. This does not attack the causal assumption, so eliminate it.

(D) No. It doesn't matter what kind of dwelling is involved. It's out of scope.

(E) Yes. Here we learn that the newsletter probably won't cause early detection, because the people who are at risk won't read it.

10. **D** This question asks what additional information we need to make the argument's conclusion true, so it's asking for an assumption. The author concludes that women make up a larger proportion of the workers in the information services industry based on his premise that a larger percentage of all women in the workforce are employed in this industry. In order for this conclusion to be true, we need to know that the corresponding percentage for men has shrunk, or that the increase in women in the information services sector is not due to growth across the entire workforce.

(A) No. Since we know that 7 percent of women in the workplace were in the information services industry, we already know that 93 percent were *not* in it, so this answer choice doesn't give us any new information.

(B) No. Retired women are out of scope.

(C) No. The specific positions of women in the industry are out of scope.

(D) Yes. If we know the percentage of male workers, we can tell whether the entire workforce has grown, or whether the corresponding percentage of men in the information services industry has shrunk.

(E) No. This is out of scope. We need to know what's happening now, not what will soon be happening.

READING COMPREHENSION DRILL

Questions 1–3

Justice is the first virtue of social institutions, as truth is of systems of thought. A theory, however elegant and eco-nomical, must be rejected or revised if it is untrue. Like-wise, laws and institutions, no matter how efficient and
5 well arranged, must be reformed or abolished if they are unjust. Each person possesses inviolability, founded on justice, which even the welfare of society as a whole cannot override. For this reason, justice denies that the loss of freedom for some is made right by a greater good
10 shared by others. It does not allow that the sacrifices imposed on a few are outweighed by the larger sum of advantages enjoyed by many.

Therefore, in a just society the liberties of equal citizenship are taken as settled; the rights secured by justice are not
15 subject to political bargaining or to the calculus of social interests. The only thing that permits us to acquiesce to an erroneous theory is the lack of a better one; analogously, an injustice is tolerable only when it is necessary to avoid an even greater injustice. As primary virtues of human activi-
20 ties, truth and justice are uncompromising.

These propositions seem to express our intuitive conviction of the primacy of justice. One might inquire whether these contentions or others similar to them are sound, and if so how they can be accounted for. To this end, it is necessary
25 to work out a theory of justice in light of which these assertions can be interpreted and assessed.

Begin by considering the role of principles of justice. Assume that a society is a more or less self-sufficient association of persons who, in their relations to one
30 another, recognize certain rules of conduct as binding and who, for the most part, act in accordance with them. Suppose further that these rules specify a system of cooperation designed to advance the good of those taking part in it. Then, although a society is a cooperative venture
35 for mutual advancement, it is typically marked by a conflict as well as by an identity of interests. There is an identity of interests since social cooperation makes possible a better

life for all than any would have if each were to live solely by his own efforts. There is a conflict of interests since
40 persons are not indifferent to how the greater benefits produced by their collaborations are distributed, for in order to pursue their ends they each prefer a larger to a lesser share.

A set of principles is required for choosing among the
45 various social arrangements that determine this division of advantages and for underwriting an agreement on the proper distributive shares. These principles are the principles of social justice: they provide a way for assigning rights and duties in the basic institutions of society and
50 they define the appropriate distribution of the benefits and burdens of social cooperation.

1. It can be inferred from the passage that the author believes that one can permit the use of an imperfect theory of justice

   ○ under no circumstances, for to do so would violate the idea of justice.
   ○ only if it would allow for the greater good of the society.
   ○ only if a more just theory cannot be found.
   ○ whenever it is agreed upon by a majority of the society.
   ○ whenever it would effectively prevent certain injustices.

2. According to the passage, a society is characterized by all of the following EXCEPT

   ○ self-sufficient individuals.
   ○ a collaborative effort for common progress.
   ○ an adherence to certain rules of behavior.
   ○ a conflict of interest among individuals.
   ○ a common interest in social cooperation

3. The author implies that, in order to ascertain whether convictions concerning the inherent nature of justice are valid, one must

○ determine the context in which they can be assessed.

○ shed light on the role of the principles of justice.

○ meet all of the requirements of a just society.

○ account for the principle of justice in society.

○ establish a theory of justice with which to evaluate them.

Questions 4–6

One of the most studied senses is vision. Scientists have carefully unraveled the connections of brain cells in the visual system and have studied how they respond to light, so we have many clues about how the brain takes visual
5 images apart. What is particularly elusive, however, is how the brain puts the pieces back together, turning two-dimensional patterns of light on the retinas into our perception of the visual world. In one case, however, the perception of color, we are beginning to get a good idea of
10 how the brain operates.

Most people think that the balance of red, green, and blue light reflected from an object into the eye determines the object's color. It is easy to demonstrate that this notion is not true, however, simply by noting that objects remain the
15 same color in daylight, fluorescent light, and incandescent light, each of which contains a mix of wavelengths of light very different from the others. Edwin Land, inventor of the instant camera, has provided an explanation of this phe-nomenon in what he calls the *retinex theory*, a term that
20 combines "retina" and "cortex" to suggest that both parts of the visual system are involved in perceiving color.

Retinex theory proposes that the retina and the cortex cooperate to perform some complex computations on the basis of light received from all areas within the visual
25 landscape. A separate computation is carried out for each of three wavelengths of light that correspond to what we

normally think of as red, green, and blue; the wavelengths
to which the three types of receptors in the retina are most
sensitive. According to the theory, the color we perceive at
30   a particular location is determined by three numbers,
computed by dividing the amount of light received from
that location at each wavelength by a weighted average of
the amount of light at that wavelength received from all
parts of the field of vision. The weighted average gives
35   more weight to light coming from close to the location in
question than to that coming from far away. The three
numbers, coordinates in a color space of three dimensions,
uniquely determine the color we see, just as the three
dimensions of physical space uniquely define the location
40   of an object. Land has conducted a number of experiments
showing that the numbers computed in this way correctly
predict what color an observer will see under a number of
unusual lighting conditions.

This remarkable theory suggests that our visual systems
45   evolved so that we see the colors of objects as the same,
regardless of the mix of wavelengths of light falling on our
retinas. Furthermore, this complex computation is carried
out virtually instantaneously without our even being aware
of it.

4.   According to the passage, the proportions of red,
     green and blue light reflected by an object cannot
     be the sole determinants of the object's color
     because

     ○   color information about three wave-
         lengths is not sufficient to produce the
         full spectrum of possible colors.
     ○   the perceived color of an object changes
         with the ambient lighting of the object's
         environment.
     ○   the image of an object is formed not by
         light coming from the object itself, but
         from other parts of the field of vision.
     ○   variations in the mix of wavelengths
         illuminating an object do not affect its
         color.
     ○   this information varies according to the
         object's proximity to the viewer.

5. The passage suggests that Edwin Land created the name *retinex* (line 19) for his optical theory in order to

○ distinguish his theory from rival theories of the retina's operation.

○ indicate that both the retina and the cortex are involved in color perception.

○ differentiate between the actions of the retina and the actions of the cortex.

○ imply that properties ascribed to the retina actually belong to the cortex.

○ indicate that the cortex and the retina work together in perceiving location.

6. It can be inferred from the passage that if the balance of red, green, and blue light entering the eye determined color, the apparent color of an object could be expected to change if the object were moved

○ from a blue background to a bright yellow background.

○ from a sunlit room to a room with fluorescent lights.

○ to a different set of coordinates in physical space.

○ close enough to take up the viewer's entire field of vision.

○ to a new area in the viewer's visual landscape.

Questions 7–9

In the early 1970s, a new system of organizing the growing acquisitions of corporations was introduced. Called the *growth/share matrix*, this tool seemed to operate on the most logical of assumptions: Corporations should sell off
5   their losing divisions as determined by the divisions' positions on the matrix, and retain and increase those divisions that the matrix considered successful.

According to the *Harvard Business Review*, the Boston Consulting Group (BCG) introduced the matrix in response

10 to corporations that had entered the heyday of acquisition
and diversification of the 1960s and early 1970s, and
subsequently faltered with the energy crisis of 1973. The
matrix worked by ordering each division according to its
position within its industry overall. Thus, managers had a
15 tool for understanding the relative success of those
businesses with whose fields they were unfamiliar. Enthusi-
asm over the matrix and its simplicity and apparent logic
obscured one of the problems inherent in the initial
situation: the wide range of acquisitions these corporations
20 had purchased.

The matrix evaluated the performance of the divisions in
terms of their competitiveness within their fields and their
cash value, but failed to analyze the relationships among
divisions that made up a corporation's holdings. For
25 instance, a corporation that owned a newspaper chain and
a paper mill would be advised to consider more than just
the relation of the paper mill's performance to that of other
mills. Beyond this, the matrix underestimated the amount
of debt a corporation could safely assume. And finally, the
30 matrix was unable to provide information regarding the
corporation's ability to manage even those successes
identified by the matrix.

Simply having a number of separately competitively
successful companies does not ensure that companies will
35 be able to support their owners without proper management and understanding. Despite the clarity and effective-
ness of the growth/share matrix as a tool for determining
divisions' performance, it could not long compensate for
the difficulties present in the initial situation it sought to
40 alleviate; that of corporations believing that their particular
management styles would function effectively for any type
of smaller business they might acquire

7. Which of the following best describes the main idea of the passage?

○ The growth/share matrix was a failure as an acquisition research tool, and hurt many corporations.

○ The growth/share matrix, though eagerly embraced at first, could not completely solve the problems it sought to address.

○ Corporations that acquire holdings that are both overly diversified and unrelated will not succeed in the business world.

○ Management style should be of primary concern when a corporation is deciding which divisions to retain and which to divest.

○ No one corporate tool can ever compensate for a lack of management skills and well–thought out acquisition planning.

8. According to the passage, all of the following were problems associated with corporations' reliance on the growth/share matrix EXCEPT

○ the overestimation by the matrix of the negative effect that debt might have on a corporation.

○ not considering divisions' relation to one another within each corporation's holdings.

○ the failure of the matrix to compensate for the lack of knowledge the corporations had about their own holdings.

○ the matrix's inability to correctly order divisions within their overall industries.

○ the matrix's lack of focus on a corporation's ability to manage its acquisitions.

9. It can be inferred from the passage that the author suggests which of the following concerning some corporations during the energy crisis of 1973?

○ The troubles of these corporations were related to problems of conforming their management styles to their new holdings.

○ Lack of fuel led many companies to have trouble powering their acquisitions.

○ Corporations' reliance on the growth/share matrix led them to mismanage their holdings.

○ Overenthusiastic buying of smaller companies left many corporations unwieldy and difficult to manage.

○ Too little diversification forced companies to find a tool to estimate the relative success of companies with whose fields they were unfamiliar.

Reading Comprehension Drill Answer Key

1.	C	6.	B
2.	A	7.	B
3.	E	8.	D
4.	D	9.	A
5.	B		

Reading Comprehension Drill Answers and Explanations

1. **C** This is a specific question, so use your key words, *imperfect theory of justice*, to skim the paragraph. You will find these words toward the end of the first paragraph. The best answer choice will paraphrase this information.

    (A) No. The author says nothing about violating the idea of justice.

    (B) No. Greater good is not mentioned in this part of the passage.

    (C) Yes. In the second-to-last sentence of the first paragraph, the author says, "The only thing that permits us to acquiesce to an erroneous theory is the lack of a better one."

    (D) No. In the first paragraph, the author says that justice "does not allow that the sacrifices imposed on a few are outweighed by the larger sum of advantages enjoyed by many."

    (E) Not quite. In the first paragraph, the author says "an injustice is tolerable *only when* it is necessary to avoid an *even greater* injustice."

2. **A** Since this is an EXCEPT question, you're looking for the answer choice that is *not true*. Those answer choices that you can support with information found in the passage should be ruled out.

    (A) Yes. A society may be self-sufficient, but the individuals within it are not.

    (B) No. The author says that the rules of a society "specify a system of cooperation designed to advance the good of those taking part in it."

(C) No. According to the passage, members of a society "recognize certain rules of conduct as binding."

(D) No. The author says, "there is a conflict of interests."

(E) No. Within a society, "social cooperation makes possible a better life for all."

3. **E** In lines 24-26, the author says, "it is necessary to work out a theory of justice in light of which these assertions can be interpreted and assessed." Eliminate all answer choices that are not a paraphrase of this idea.

(A) No. Context is not discussed here.

(B) No. This concept is discussed much earlier in the passage.

(C) No. "All" is extreme wording. Eliminate it.

(D) No. Justice in society is discussed later in the passage.

(E) Yes. This is a paraphrase of what the author contends in lines 24-26

4. **D** Your key words are *proportions of red, green, and blue light*. Skim until you find these words in the passage (at the beginning of the second paragraph, slightly rephrased) and read around them.

(A) No. The passage does not say this anywhere.

(B) No. This is the exact *opposite* of the correct answer. You read about the mistaken notion that the "balance of red, green, and blue light" determines an object's color. The next sentence states that this notion is untrue *because* an object's color stays the *same* regardless of the ambient lighting.

(C) No. The passage says that light from other parts of the field of vision is *part* of the calculation, but that light coming from the object itself is still central. Furthermore, this idea is discussed in the third paragraph, and you should not be looking there for the answer to this question.

(D) Yes. This is a great paraphrase of the second sentence of the second paragraph, which says that objects remain the same color in daylight, fluorescent light, and incandescent light.

(E) No. The issue of the object's proximity to the viewer only comes up in the third paragraph (as part of the retinex theory computation).

5. **B** Go to the lines indicated in the questions and start reading about one sentence before it. Stop about one sentence after the lines referenced. You should find your answer, that "both parts of the visual system are involved in perceiving color." A good answer will restate that definition.

(A) No. The question specifically asks for a reason for the *name*.

(B) Yes. Line 20 states that the term combines the two words "to suggest that both parts" are involved.

(C) No. The passage never emphasizes differentiating the two

(D) No. The passage only states that both retina and cortex are involved, it does not ascribe specific properties to either one.

(E) No. Read carefully—*location* is not what this theory is about. It's about color perception.

6. **B** This question is tricky. Use the lead words to take you to the first two sentences of the second paragraph. These sentences tell you that objects stay the same color despite different ambient lighting.

(A) No. The actual *color* of a background is not discussed so you can't infer anything about it.

(B) Yes. The answer to this question depends on lines 14-17—specifically the information that daylight, fluorescent light, and incandescent light each contain a mix of wavelengths of light very different from the others.

(C) No. The object's location is discussed in the third paragraph and is not relevant to this question.

(D) No. The object's distance from the viewer is not relevant to this question.

(E) No. Where the object is in the viewer's visual field is not relevant to this question.

7. **B** The best way to answer this general question, since it comes prior to any specific questions, is to skim the first sentences of each paragraph and the last sentence of the passage as a whole. You will determine that the passage is about a new system for organizing the growing acquisitions (first paragraph), that it's called the growth/share matrix and it obscured a problem (second paragraph), and that, despite its usefulness, there were too many difficulties with it (last sentence).

(A) No. This is extreme. The passage does not go as far as to term the matrix a failure.

(B) Yes. This accurately states the message of the passage.

(C) No. This judgment is outside the scope of the passage.

(D) No. Management style is outside the scope of the passage.

(E) No. This is extreme, and outside the scope of the passage.

8. **D** Since this is an EXCEPT question, keep in mind that four answer choices address the question, and the fifth one, which does not, is the credited response. This question also applies to the passage as a whole, so use each answer choice as your lead words.

(A) No. Negative debt was discussed in the second paragraph of the passage.

(B) No. Divisions' relations to each other were also discussed in the second paragraph.

(C) No. Lack of knowledge was addressed at the end of the first paragraph: "managers had a tool for understanding the relative success of those businesses with whose fields they were unfamiliar."

(D) Yes. "Inability to correctly order division" was never mentioned as a problem in the passage, and so is a good answer for an EXCEPT question.

(E) No. This is summarized in the last sentence of the passage.

9. **A** Read closely around the words *energy crisis of 1973*. Remember that the credited response *must* be a paraphrase. Refer to the passage if you need to.

(A) Yes. This is stated in the final sentence of the passage.

(B) No. This answer choice confuses two notions of "powering."

(C) No. Mismanagement due to the growth/share matrix and the matrix itself only came into play after 1973.

(D) This is never specifically related to the energy crisis of 1973.

(E) No. The problem was not one of the *lack* of diversification, but rather too much.

MATH DRILLS

PROBLEM SOLVING DRILL

1. If $\dfrac{.036 \times 10^a}{.09 \times 10^b} = 4 \times 10^5$, then $a - b = ?$

   - ○ 7
   - ○ 6
   - ○ 5
   - ○ 4
   - ○ 3

2.

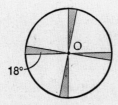

   In order to create a part for a certain piece of machinery, four equal-size wedge-shaped pieces are cut and removed from a circular piece of metal, as illustrated in the diagram above. If the unshaded portion of the circle represents the material remaining after the pieces are removed, what percentage of the original circle remains?

   - ○ 10
   - ○ 20
   - ○ 25
   - ○ 60
   - ○ 80

3. $\left(2+\sqrt{7}\right)\left(2-\sqrt{7}\right) =$

- ○ $-3-4\sqrt{7}$
- ○ -3
- ○ -1

- ○ $4-4\sqrt{7}$
- ○ 11

4. The number of cells killed by a virus doubles every hour. If the number of cells killed was initially 10^3, what is the number of cells killed after an additional seven hours have passed?

- ○ $8\left(10^3\right)$

- ○ $\left(10^3\right)\left(10^8\right)$

- ○ $2^8\left(10^3\right)$

- ○ $2^4\left(10^3\right)$

- ○ $2^8\left(10^8\right)$

5. For all numbers m and n, $m \Diamond n = \dfrac{m^2\left(m-n\right)}{n^2}$.

What is $3 \Diamond 2$?

- ○ $\dfrac{1}{2}$

- ○ $\dfrac{9}{4}$

○ $\frac{3}{2}$

○ 3

○ 9

6. In a certain egg-processing plant, every egg must be inspected, and is either accepted for processing or is rejected. For every 96 eggs accepted for processing, 4 eggs are rejected. If, on a particular day, 12 additional eggs were accepted, but the overall number of eggs inspected remained the same, the ratio of those accepted to those rejected would be 99 to 1. How many eggs does the plant process per day?

○ 100
○ 300
○ 400
○ 3,000
○ 4,000

7. In a 5-hour race, 6 cars consumed 480 gallons of gas between them. Assuming a constant rate of consumption, how much gas would be consumed by 7 cars in an 8-hour race?

○ 560
○ 654.5
○ 768
○ 864
○ 896

8. If a golfer scores an average of p points per round of golf for r rounds, and then scores q points in his next round, what is the golfer's average score for the $\left(r+1\right)$ rounds of golf?

○ $\dfrac{pr+q}{r+1}$

○ $p\left(\dfrac{r+q}{r+1}\right)$

○ $p+2$

○ $p+4$

○ $p+12$

9. In the rectangular coordinate system, the line $2y-3x=14$ passes through each of the four quadrants EXCEPT

○ I

○ II

○ IV

○ I and IV

○ II and IV

10. Of the 140 moving trucks available to rent, 82 have air conditioning, 56 have automatic transmission, and 24 trucks have both air conditioning and automatic transmission. How many of the 140 trucks have neither air conditioning nor automatic transmission?

○ 4

○ 16

○ 26

○ 28

○ 32

11. On a certain day, a delivery driver must make 4 deliveries. He departs from the dispatch office and travels 14 miles due west to his first delivery. From there, his second delivery is 7 miles due north, and his third delivery is 9 miles due east of the location of his second delivery. His last delivery is 19 miles due south of his third. Assuming the terrain is flat, what is the distance, in miles, that the driver must travel to return to the dispatch office, if he travels in a straight line via the shortest route?

○ 33
○ 17
○ 13
○ 7
○ It cannot be determined from the information given.

12. A 6-sided die has 3 black sides and 3 white sides. If the die is thrown 4 times, what is the probability that, on at least one of the throws, the die will land with a black side up?

○ $\dfrac{1}{16}$

○ $\dfrac{3}{16}$

○ $\dfrac{1}{2}$

○ $\dfrac{9}{16}$

○ $\dfrac{15}{16}$

13. A caterer must choose 3 canapés to serve from 12 possible selections. In how many possible combinations can he serve the 3 canapés?

   ○ 220
   ○ 440
   ○ 660
   ○ 1100
   ○ 1320

14. A group of 10 coworkers has agreed to equally share the cost of a gift costing d dollars. If w of the coworkers later decide not to contribute, how much more must each of the remaining coworkers pay toward the gift?

   ○ $\dfrac{d}{10-w}$

   ○ $\dfrac{d(w-10)}{10w}$

   ○ $\dfrac{dw}{10(10-w)}$

   ○ $\dfrac{10-w}{d}$

   ○ $\dfrac{10dw}{10-w}$

15. A merchant prices a television at 60 percent above wholesale. For a President's Day sale, the merchant marks the television down by 25 percent. If he sells the television during the President's Day sale, what percentage over the wholesale price will he have earned?

   ○ 75
   ○ 50
   ○ 35
   ○ 25
   ○ 20

Problem Solving Drill Answer Key

1.	**B**	6.	**C**	11.	**C**
2.	**E**	7.	**E**	12.	**E**
3.	**B**	8.	**A**	13.	**A**
4.	**C**	9.	**C**	14.	**C**
5.	**B**	10.	**C**	15.	**E**

Problem Solving Drill Answers and Explanations

1. **B** If $\dfrac{.036 \times 10^a}{.09 \times 10^b} = 4 \times 10^5$, then you'll have to manipulate the equation in such a way as to end up with a 4 and a 10^5. So start by separating the equation into two parts, $\dfrac{.036}{.09} \times \dfrac{10^a}{10^b}$, and focus on the nonexponent part first. You know that $\dfrac{36}{9} = 4$, but you need to get rid of the decimals before you can get there. Multiply the fraction by $\dfrac{1,000}{1,000}$, which gives you

    $\dfrac{1000}{1000} \times \dfrac{.036}{.09} = \dfrac{36}{9 \times 10} = 4 \times \dfrac{1}{10}$. So you have the "4" part.

    Now work on the exponents. You have $4 \times \dfrac{1}{10} \times \dfrac{10^a}{10^b}$. Combine the fractions to get $\dfrac{10^a}{10^{b+1}}$, which you know equals 10^5. Simplify the fraction to $10^{(a-b+1)}$. Since $10^{(a-b+1)} = 10^5$, $a - b + 1 = 5$, and $a - b = 4$.

2. **E** When you are asked to find a shaded portion of a circle, you have to figure out what fractional portion of the circle's 360° you're talking about. You know that the shaded portions of the circle have angles of 18° and that there are 4 of them. In

essence, you are talking about $\left(\dfrac{18 \times 4}{360}\right)$, which is $\dfrac{72}{360}$, or $\dfrac{1}{5}$ of

the circle. This leaves $\dfrac{4}{5}$, and that's 80 percent.

3. **B** You should use FOIL on a problem like this one.

$$\text{First: } 2 \times 2 = 4$$

$$\text{Outer: } 2 \times -\sqrt{7} = -2\sqrt{7}$$

$$\text{Inner: } 2 \times \sqrt{7} = 2\sqrt{7}$$

$$\text{Last: } \sqrt{7} \times -\sqrt{7} = -7$$

$$4 - 2\sqrt{7} + 2\sqrt{7} - 7 = 4 - 7 = -3$$

4. **C** If at the zero hour, you have 1×10^3 virus cells, and the number doubles every hour, then after the first hour, you have 2×10^3. As you proceed, keep in mind what the answer choices look like—you don't need to multiply anything out. After the second hour you have $2^2 \times 10^3$, and so on. At the end of the eighth hour, you have $2^8 \times 10^3$ cells.

5. **B** It's a function problem, so everywhere you see an m in the original, put 3, and where you see an n, put 2.

$$3 \lozenge 2 = \dfrac{3^2(3-2)}{2^2} = \dfrac{9(1)}{4} = \dfrac{9}{4}$$

6. **C** The ratio of accepted to rejected eggs is 96:4. So for every 100 eggs, 4 are rejected and 96 are accepted. When 12 more eggs are accepted, the ratio shifts to 99 accepted and 1 rejected, which means that for every 100 eggs, 3 more are accepted and 3 fewer rejected. If, for every 100 eggs, 3 more are accepted, then for 12 more to be accepted using the same ratio, the plant must process 400 eggs ($3 \times 4 = 12$).

7. **E** This is a work problem in disguise. You first need to figure out how much gas one car consumes in one hour, so divide the total by the number of cars, and then the number of hours.

$$\dfrac{480}{6} = 80$$

$$\frac{80}{5} = 16$$

So each car consumes 16 gallons of gas per hour, and in an 8-hour race, 7 cars would consume $16 \times 8 \times 7$, or 896 gallons.

8. **A** Plug in. If the golfer averages 90 (p) points per round, and he plays 4 (r) rounds, and then gets a 100 (q) on his next round, then his average score for the 5 games would look like this:

$$Average = \frac{Total}{Number}$$

$$Average = \frac{(90 \times 4) + 100}{4 + 1}$$

$$Average = \frac{(360) + 100}{5}$$

$$Average = \frac{460}{5} = 92$$

Be careful and check all the answer choices; otherwise you might choose (D) $p + 2$. Choice (D) happens to be the answer for *this* set of numbers, but the real answer is choice (A). Remember, if you plug in and get two answer choices that work, simply plug in another set of numbers, and check only the two remaining answer choices.

9. **C** To graph a line, its equation must be in the form $y = mx + b$. Manipulate the equation you were given, $2y - 3x = 14$ until you have isolated y on one side of the equation.

$$2y - 3x = 14$$

$$2y = 14 + 3x$$

$$y = \frac{14 + 3x}{2}$$

$$y = \frac{14}{2} + \frac{3}{2}x$$

$$y = 7 + \frac{3}{2}x$$

$$y = \frac{3}{2}x + 7$$

So the slope of the line is $\frac{3}{2}$ and the y-intercept is 7. Sketch the coordinate grid on your scratch paper and plot in the y-intercept at 7.

Now plot the second point using the slope. Slope is $\frac{rise}{run}$ so count 3 up and 2 over to the right. (If the slope were negative, you would count 2 over to the left). Connect the points and draw your line

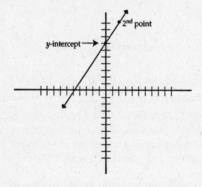

Your line passes through Quadrant I, II, and III, but not IV.

10. **C**   This is a group problem, so use the formula
$Total = Group_1 + Group_2 - Both + Neither$

The total is 140, Group 1 is trucks with air conditioning (82), Group 2 is trucks with automatic transmission (56), and 24 trucks have both. Plug in what you know and solve for "Neither":

$$140 = 82 + 56 - 24 + Neither$$

$$140 = 114 + Neither$$

$$140 - 114 = Neither$$

$$26 = Neither$$

11. **C** With a problem like this, when there is no diagram, go ahead and draw one. To get from the last stop back to the dispatch office, the shortest route is a diagonal line, as shown in the diagram. The diagonal line is also the hypotenuse of a right triangle, and the measurements of the two sides of that triangle are 5 and 12, as shown below.

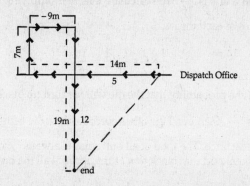

To find the length of the hypotenuse of a right triangle, use the Pythagorean Theorem.

$$a^2 + b^2 = c^2$$

$$5^2 + 12^2 = c^2$$

$$25 + 144 = c^2$$

$$169 = c^2$$

$$\sqrt{169} = c$$

$$13 = c$$

So the distance is 13 miles.

12. **E** The probability of the die landing with a black side up on any one throw is $\frac{1}{2}$. The question asks for the probability that the die will land black side up on at least 1 out of 4 throws. This represents a lot of combinations.

It is quicker to think of it this way—the only outcome in which the die is *not* black side up at least once out of 4 throws is when all 4 throws are white. The probability of all 4 throws turning up white is $\frac{1}{16}$. You calculate this by multiplying the probabilities of each throw.

$$\frac{1}{2} \times \frac{1}{2} \times \frac{1}{2} \times \frac{1}{2} = \frac{1}{16}$$

If the probability that the die will *not* turn up black at least once is $\frac{1}{16}$, then in all the other outcomes, the die turns up black at least once. The total of all outcomes is always 1, so subtract the likelihood that black *won't* turn up from all the outcomes:

$$1 - \frac{1}{16} = \frac{15}{16}$$

So the probability that black will turn up on at least one of the four throws is $\frac{15}{16}$.

13. **A** This is a combination problem—one in which order does not matter. Use the formula $C = \dfrac{n!}{r!(n-r)!}$, in which n is the total number of things you're choosing from and r is the number you're choosing.

$$n = 12 \text{ and } r = 3$$

$$C = \frac{12!}{3!(12-3)!}$$
$$C = \frac{12!}{3!(9!)}$$

At this point, start reducing.

$$C = \frac{12 \times 11 \times 10}{3 \times 2 \times 1} = 2 \times 11 \times 10 = 220$$

If you used the formula for permutations, you got 1,320.

14. **C**   This is a classic Plugging In problem. Try using 100 for the cost of the gift, and 2 for the number of coworkers who drop out. If 8 coworkers split the cost of the gift, it costs them each $12.50, which is $2.50 more than they had originally planned to pay.

Plug the same numbers into the answer choices, and you'll find (C) works. If you chose (A), that's the total amount each now pays, and the question wants only the increased amount.

15. **E**   This is also a Plugging In problem—your answer choices are all percentages, so they are really variables. Use $100 for the wholesale price of the television. The merchant marks it up 60 percent, or $60, which makes the price $160. He them reduces that price by 25 percent. 25 percent of $160 is $40, which makes the President's Day sale price $120. The merchant makes $20 on the sale, which is 20 percent of the original price.

Data Sufficiency Drill

Directions: Data Sufficiency problems consist of a question and two statements, labeled (1) and (2), in which certain data are given. You have to decide whether the data given in the statements are <u>sufficient</u> for answering the question. Using the data given in the statements plus your knowledge of mathematics and everyday facts (such as the number of days in July or the meaning of *counterclockwise*), you are to fill in oval

- ○   if statement (1) ALONE is sufficient, but statement (2) alone is not sufficient.
- ○   if statement (2) ALONE is sufficient, but statement (1) alone is not sufficient.
- ○   if both statements together are sufficient, but NEITHER statement ALONE is sufficient.
- ○   EACH statement ALONE is sufficient.
- ○   statements (1) and (2) together are NOT sufficient.

1.   If $2^x(7^y) = z$, what is the value of z?

    1. $x - y = 1$
    2. $2^x = 8$

- ○   Statement (1) ALONE is sufficient, but statement (2) alone is not sufficient.
- ○   Statement (2) ALONE is sufficient, but statement (1) alone is not sufficient.
- ○   Both statements together are sufficient, but NEITHER statement ALONE is sufficient.
- ○   EACH statement ALONE is sufficient.
- ○   Statements (1) and (2) together are NOT sufficient.

2. In the Reagan High School swim club, 120 members swim the backstroke or the crawl or both. If 30 of these members do not swim the backstroke, how many members swim both the crawl and the backstroke?

   1. Of the 120 members, 72 do not swim the crawl.
   2. A total of 48 members swim the crawl.

   ○ Statement (1) ALONE is sufficient, but statement (2) alone is not sufficient.
   ○ Statement (2) ALONE is sufficient, but statement (1) alone is not sufficient.
   ○ Both statements together are sufficient, but NEITHER statement ALONE is sufficient.
   ○ EACH statement ALONE is sufficient.
   ○ Statements (1) and (2) together are NOT sufficient.

3. If p and q are integers, is $p + q$ odd?

   1. $\dfrac{p}{3}$ is not an odd integer.
   2. $p - q$ is an even integer.

   ○ Statement (1) ALONE is sufficient, but statement (2) alone is not sufficient.
   ○ Statement (2) ALONE is sufficient, but statement (1) alone is not sufficient.
   ○ Both statements together are sufficient, but NEITHER statement ALONE is sufficient.
   ○ EACH statement ALONE is sufficient.
   ○ Statements (1) and (2) together are NOT sufficient.

4. At the beginning of last year, a furniture store had 75 armchairs in stock, which had cost the store $600 each. During the same year, the store purchased a number of additional armchairs. What is the total amount spent by the store on the armchairs it had in stock at the end of last year?

   1. Last year, the store purchased 30 armchairs for $500 each.
   2. Last year, the total revenue from the sale of armchairs was $16,500.

   ○ Statement (1) ALONE is sufficient, but statement (2) alone is not sufficient.
   ○ Statement (2) ALONE is sufficient, but statement (1) alone is not sufficient.
   ○ Both statements together are sufficient, but NEITHER statement ALONE is sufficient.
   ○ EACH statement ALONE is sufficient.
   ○ Statements (1) and (2) together are NOT sufficient.

5. What is the ratio of the number of boys to girls on the school bus?

   1. The number of boys is 5 less than twice the number of girls.
   2. The difference between the number of boys and the number of girls is 35.

   ○ Statement (1) ALONE is sufficient, but statement (2) alone is not sufficient.
   ○ Statement (2) ALONE is sufficient, but statement (1) alone is not sufficient.
   ○ Both statements together are sufficient, but NEITHER statement ALONE is sufficient.
   ○ EACH statement ALONE is sufficient.
   ○ Statements (1) and (2) together are NOT sufficient.

6. How long did it take Bob to complete the race?

1. If Bob were $\frac{2}{3}$ faster, his time would have been 3 hours.
2. Bob's average speed was 30 miles per hour.

○ Statement (1) ALONE is sufficient, but statement (2) alone is not sufficient.
○ Statement (2) ALONE is sufficient, but statement (1) alone is not sufficient.
○ Both statements together are sufficient, but NEITHER statement ALONE is sufficient.
○ EACH statement ALONE is sufficient.
○ Statements (1) and (2) together are NOT sufficient.

7.

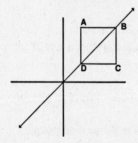

In the rectangular coordinate system above, is ABCD a square?

1. Points C and D both have y-coordinates of 3.
2. ∠ABD = 45°

○ Statement (1) ALONE is sufficient, but statement (2) alone is not sufficient.
○ Statement (2) ALONE is sufficient, but statement (1) alone is not sufficient.
○ Both statements together are sufficient, but NEITHER statement ALONE is sufficient.
○ EACH statement ALONE is sufficient.
○ Statements (1) and (2) together are NOT sufficient.

8. $K = \dfrac{\dfrac{r}{3}}{\dfrac{p+2}{p^2-2p-r^2}}$. What is the value

of K?

1. $r = 2p$
2. $p = 5$, and $2r - 2p = 2p$

○ Statement (1) ALONE is sufficient, but statement (2) alone is not sufficient.
○ Statement (2) ALONE is sufficient, but statement (1) alone is not sufficient.
○ Both statements together are sufficient, but NEITHER statement ALONE is sufficient.
○ EACH statement ALONE is sufficient.
○ Statements (1) and (2) together are NOT sufficient.

9. A drawer contains 12 socks, of which 8 are black and 4 are white. If 3 of the socks are removed, how many of the socks that remain in the drawer are black?

1. The socks that remain in the drawer have a ratio of 2 black to 1 white.
2. One of the first two socks removed is black.

○ Statement (1) ALONE is sufficient, but statement (2) alone is not sufficient.
○ Statement (2) ALONE is sufficient, but statement (1) alone is not sufficient.
○ Both statements together are sufficient, but NEITHER statement ALONE is sufficient.
○ EACH statement ALONE is sufficient.
○ Statements (1) and (2) together are NOT sufficient.

10.

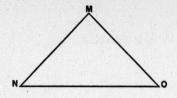

Is *MNO* a right triangle?

1. $\overline{MN} = 2\sqrt{2}$

2. $\angle MNO = \angle MON = \dfrac{1}{2}\angle OMN$

○ Statement (1) ALONE is sufficient, but statement (2) alone is not sufficient.

○ Statement (2) ALONE is sufficient, but statement (1) alone is not sufficient.

○ Both statements together are sufficient, but NEITHER statement ALONE is sufficient.

○ EACH statement ALONE is sufficient.

○ Statements (1) and (2) together are NOT sufficient.

11. Train A leaves the station at 5:00, and travels north at 50 miles per hour. If train B leaves the same station some time later, heading in the same direction as train A, at what time will train B overtake train A?

1. Train B leaves the station at 6:00.

2. Train A travels at $\dfrac{5}{6}$ the speed of train B.

○ Statement (1) ALONE is sufficient, but statement (2) alone is not sufficient.

○ Statement (2) ALONE is sufficient, but statement (1) alone is not sufficient.

○ Both statements together are sufficient, but NEITHER statement ALONE is sufficient.

○ EACH statement ALONE is sufficient.

○ Statements (1) and (2) together are NOT sufficient.

12. If e is an integer, is $\dfrac{1}{2^e}$ greater than or less than 1?

1. $-e < 1$

2. $e^2 > 0$

○ Statement (1) ALONE is sufficient, but statement (2) alone is not sufficient.

○ Statement (2) ALONE is sufficient, but statement (1) alone is not sufficient.

○ Both statements together are sufficient, but NEITHER statement ALONE is sufficient.

○ EACH statement ALONE is sufficient.

○ Statements (1) and (2) together are NOT sufficient.

Data Sufficiency Drill Answer Key

1.	C	6.	A	11.	C
2.	D	7.	E	12.	A
3.	B	8.	B		
4.	E	9.	A		
5.	C	10.	B		

Data Sufficiency Drill Answers and Explanations

1. **C** Your first instinct here should be to think that statements (1) and (2) together are sufficient to determine the values of x and y, because as long as you have the same number of variables as you have equations, the data are sufficient. But in this case, one of the equations has an exponent, which means you need to work through the problem.

    So there's one equation in (1) and one in (2)—you have two equations. Using them together, you can define x and y, which then allows you to solve for z. Start with statement (1). It does not give you enough information, so write BCE on your scratch paper. Now take statement (2). If $2^x = 8$, then $x = 3$. Statement (2) alone is not sufficient, so cross off (B). You can take $x = 3$ and substitute it into the equation in statement (1), and that means that statement (1) and statement (2) together are sufficient to solve for x and y. With the values for x and y, you could determine the value of z.

2. **D** This is essentially a group problem, but nowhere in the problem do you have information about the "Neither" part of the group. This might lead you to hastily (and incorrectly) choose (E) as the answer. In fact, you have plenty of information.

    The question is asking about Group 1 (members who swim the backstroke), Group 2 (members who swim the crawl), and Both (members who swim both), so just use that part of the formula:

    $$\text{Group}_1 + \text{Group}_2 - \text{Both} = 120$$

You know that 30 members do not swim the backstroke, which means that they swim only the crawl. Fill that in, so that you have:

$$\text{Group}_1 + 30 - \text{Both} = 120$$

Now proceed to the statements. You need only the numbers for either Group 1 or Both.

Statement (1) tells you that 72 members do not swim the crawl. These are the members who swim only the backstroke—Group 1. Statement (1) is sufficient, so write down *AD*. Statement (2) gives you the number of people who swim the crawl, which encompasses the 30 members in Group 2 plus the members who swim Both. This means there are 18 members who swim both strokes, and statement (2) alone is sufficient, so the answer is (D).

3. **B** On yes/no questions with variables, you have to plug into the statements twice. Try plugging in 6 and 2 for p and q the first time. Using statement (1), you find that $p = 6$ is not sufficient, so write down *BCE*. Plugging the same numbers; 6 and 2, into statement (2) works, so try them on the question. This is enough information, so statement (2) alone is sufficient this time.

Now choose another set of numbers to Plug In. Try 0 and –2, and start with statement (2), because if it is still sufficient by itself, your answer is (B). And it is.

4. **E** To answer this question, you need to know how many arm-chairs the store sold and how many additional armchairs were purchased and what they cost. Statement (1) tells you the cost of the additional armchairs purchased, but is not sufficient, so write *BCE*. Statement (2) gives you a total without the number of armchairs it encompasses, so it is not sufficient. Cross off (B). Together the statements do not give you enough information.

5. **C** Two equations, two variables. Statement (1) can be rewritten as $b = 2g - 5$ and statement (2) can be written as $b - g = 35$. Alone, neither equation is sufficient, but together they are.

6. **A** Use the distance 3 formula for this one. $r \times t = d$. Plug in the number you know:

$$\frac{5}{3}r = 3 = d$$

$$rt = 5r$$

$$t = 5$$

(A) is sufficient to answer the question so eliminate (B), (C), (D) and (E). Now look at statement (2). Knowing Bob's rate alone will not help you determine how long it took him to complete the race, so the answer is (A).

7. **E** In order for a quadrilateral to be a square, it must have 4 equal sides and 4 equal angles of 90°. So you'll need to know the lengths of the sides and the angle measurements.

   Redraw the diagram on your scratch paper, and label everything you know. Statement (1) tell you that points C and D have y-coordinates of 3, but this does not work alone, so write BCE. Statement (2) tells you that the angle formed by the diagonal is 45°, but this does not tell you the measurement of $\angle DBC$, or any other angle, for that matter. So statement (2) alone is not sufficient. Even taken together, statement (1) and statement (2) do not tell you the lengths of the sides or the measure of the angles of the quadrilateral, so the data are not sufficient.

8. **B** You need two equations, because you have 2 variables. Statement (1) gives you only one. But statement (2) gives you two equations, and from that information, you can determine the values of p and q (and therefore K, but don't waste your time with K—remember, you don't have to solve). So statement (2) alone is sufficient.

9. **A** This question looks like a probability question, but is actually simpler than that. Start with statement (1). By removing 3 of the 12 socks, you have reduced the number of socks in the drawer to 9. Statement (1) tells you the socks remaining in the drawer have a ratio of 2 to 1, so you have 6 black and 3 white socks. This answers the question, and statement (1) is sufficient, so write down *AD*.

   Statement (2) tells you one of the first 2 socks removed is black, but tells you nothing about what's left or what else you removed, so it is not sufficient. The answer is (A).

10. **B** Statement (1) tells you the length of the hypotenuse, and while it looks like a typical measurement of the hypotenuse of a right triangle, statement (1) is not sufficient to guarantee this is a right triangle. Write down *BCE*.

Statement (2) gives you all the information you need: the angles in a triangle add up to 180°, and you know the relationship of all three angles to each other. If you went ahead and solved using statement (2), you'd learn that the triangle has two 45° angles and one 90° angle. But why waste your time, when you know that statement (2) alone is sufficient?

11. **C** There are a couple of different ways to crack this problem, but perhaps the most straightforward is for you to just reason through it—no algebra necessary. Train A is chugging along at a leisurely 50 mph. In order for train B to overtake train A, it simply has to be travelling faster than 50 mph. We don't care how long it actually takes; *we only care whether we could figure out how long it takes, if we had to.*

Statement (1) tells you what time train B leaves the station. This does not tell us whether train B is faster than train A, so it is not sufficient. Write down *BCE*. Statement (2) tells us that train B is faster than train A, so statement (2) and statement (1) are sufficient—the answer is C.

12. **A** Start with statement (1) and try plugging in 2, because $-2 < 1$. If e is 2, then $\frac{1}{2^e} = \frac{1}{2^2} = \frac{1}{4}$. So, in this case, the answer to the question is yes. Now plug in a negative number. Try -2. It does not work. In fact, only positive integers can be plugged into statement (1), so you know that statement (1) is sufficient. Write down *AD*.

Go to statement (2), and plug in 2 again. Yes, $2^2 > 0$. Plug 2 into the question. You know this works, because it worked in for statement (1) and gave you the answer of yes. So with positive integers, statement (2) is also sufficient.

What about negative numbers? Try -2 in statement (2). Yes, $(-2)^2 > 0$. But when you plug -2 into the question, you get $\frac{1}{2^{-2}} = 4$, which is not less than 1, so the answer is no, and statement (2) alone turns out not to be sufficient. The answer is A.

About the Author

Cathryn Still received a bachelor's degree from Trinity University and a master's from The University of Texas. She joined The Princeton Review in 1990, starting as a teacher, and ultimately moved into Management, where she has served as Managing Director of Graduate Programs since 1997.

NOTES

NOTES

NOTES

NOTES

NOTES

NOTES

Expert Advice

www.review.com

Talk About It

www.review.com

Pop Surveys

Paying for it

www.review.com

THE PRINCETON REVIEW

Getting in

Word du Jour

Find-O-Rama School & Career Search

www.review.com

Best Schools

Finding it

www.review.com

FIND US...

International

Hong Kong
4/F Sun Hung Kai Centre
30 Harbour Road, Wan Chai,
Hong Kong
Tel: (011)85-2-517-3016

Japan
Fuji Building 40, 15-14
Sakuragaokacho, Shibuya Ku,
Tokyo 150, Japan
Tel: (011)81-3-3463-1343

Korea
Tae Young Bldg, 944-24,
Daechi- Dong, Kangnam-Ku
The Princeton Review- ANC
Seoul, Korea 135-280,
South Korea
Tel: (011)82-2-554-7763

Mexico City
PR Mex S De RL De Cv
Guanajuato 228 Col. Roma
06700 Mexico D.F., Mexico
Tel: 525-564-9468

Montreal
666 Sherbrooke St.
West, Suite 202
Montreal, QC H3A 1E7 Canada
Tel: (514) 499-0870

Pakistan
1 Bawa Park - 90 Upper Mall
Lahore, Pakistan
Tel: (011)92-42-571-2315

Spain
Pza. Castilla, 3 - 5° A, 28046
Madrid, Spain
Tel: (011)341-323-4212

Taiwan
155 Chung Hsiao East Road
Section 4 - 4th Floor,
Taipei R.O.C., Taiwan
Tel: (011)886-2-751-1243

Thailand
Building One, 99 Wireless Road
Bangkok, Thailand 10330
Tel: (662) 256-7080

Toronto
1240 Bay Street, Suite 300
Toronto M5R 2A7 Canada
Tel: (800) 495-7737
Tel: (716) 839-4391

Vancouver
4212 University Way NE,
Suite 204
Seattle, WA 98105
Tel: (206) 548-1100

National (U.S.)

We have over 60 offices around the U.S. and
run courses in over 400 sites. For courses and locations
within the U.S. call 1 (800) 2/Review and you will be
routed to the nearest office.